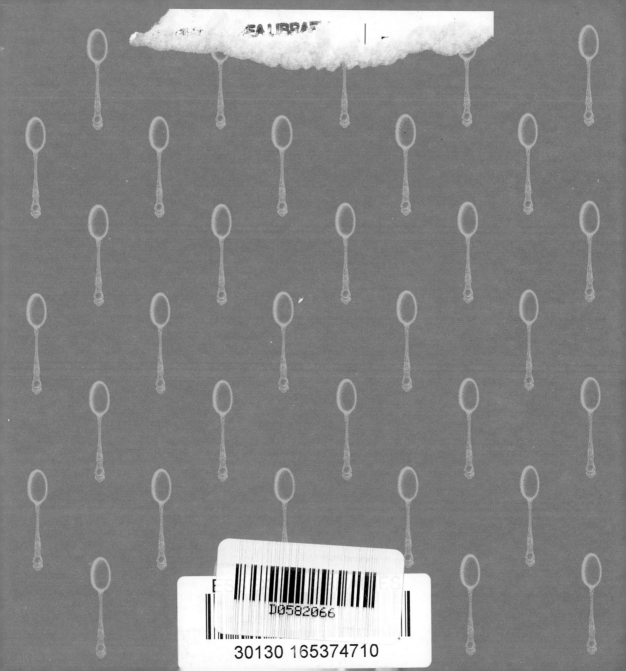

GOOD OLD-FASHIONED
CAKES

GOOD OLD-FASHIONED
CAKES

Jane Pettigrew

First published in the United Kingdom in 2010 by
National Trust Books
10 Southcombe Street
London
W14 0RA

An imprint of Anova Books Company Ltd

Recipes sourced from *Traditional Teatime Recipes*, published by National Trust Books, 2007

ISBN: 9781905400898

A CIP catalogue record for this book is available from the British Library.

18 17 16 15 14 13 12 10
10 9 8 7 6 5 4 3 2 1

Reproduction by Dot Gradations Ltd, UK
Printed by Toppan Leefung Printing Ltd, China

This book can be ordered direct from the publisher at the website www.anovabooks.com,
or try your local bookshop. Also available at National Trust shops and www.nationaltrustbooks.co.uk.

CONTENTS

INTRODUCTION

All over Britain today, the growing popularity of afternoon tea is evident in hotel tea lounges, tea bars and tearooms. Up and down the country, waiters and waitresses scurry to and fro, taking orders for pots of Darjeeling, Assam, Ceylon and Jasmine tea and delivering to the tables silver cake stands and pretty porcelain dishes laden with elegant pastries, cream-filled slices of irresistible gateaux and little fruit tartlets that tempt with their toppings of scarlet, pink and purple currants and berries. And although we have less leisure time than our Victorian and Edwardian ancestors, tea parties at home are still a wonderfully social way of celebrating a birthday, getting to know new neighbours or gathering friends together for a relaxed and uninterrupted chat.

The first afternoon teas were enjoyed in aristocratic households in the 1840s and included little more than pots of tea served with thinly sliced bread and butter. But as the fashion grew, ladies took to creating more elaborate menus and introduced a wider choice of sweet treats. By 1861, in her renowned *Book of Household Management*, Isabella Beeton included 25 pages of recipes for biscuits, buns, crumpets, muffins and cakes but these were, on the whole, rather plain and modest in both their ingredients and their names. She gave instructions for making Light Buns and Good Plain Buns, Crisp Biscuits and Simple

Hard Biscuits, and her cake recipes included Common Cake, Economical Cake, A Nice Useful Cake, Good Holiday Cake and Common Seed Cake – all of which sound rather unappetising and dull. As different tea meals became more and more popular, recipe books added fancier creations – strawberry chocolate cakes, light-as-a-feather Victoria sponges sandwiched together with butter-cream fillings, Queen Cake, Imperial gingerbreads, rich butter shortbreads and Prince Albert Cake flavoured with cinnamon, cloves and raisins.

Baking in those days was a much longer and more laborious occupation. For a family fruit cake, sultanas, currants and raisins were first rubbed with flour to help separate the lumps, any stalks and pieces of grit were removed, and the fruit was then carefully washed in cold water, drained, spread on a soft cloth and gently squeezed to remove the water. Finally, it was spread out in a baking dish and dried in the oven. Other ingredients too needed careful preparation. Flour had to be carefully sifted to remove any hard lumps and fibre; butter had to be washed free of salt and squeezed in a muslin cloth to remove any water or buttermilk; spices had to be grated by hand; sugar was delivered in hard cones which had to be broken, pounded and sieved to make a powder fine enough for mixing into cakes and pies, and any beating had to be done by hand with wooden spoons. Gradually the cook's life became easier with the introduction of electricity, new labour-saving gadgets and the availability of refined sugar that needed less pounding, and a new milling system that removed bran and wheatgerm from flour and produced lighter, fluffier cakes and breads. One company offered 'Aerated' flour that contained soda or pearl ash (purified potassium carbonate) as raising agents and claimed that the advantages included 'the large amount of time saved in the preparation; the marvellous value of its digestive properties and the acknowledged superiority over all other makes'.

During the first half of the 19th century, many homes still cooked on an open fire and this limited the types of cakes that could be prepared. Griddle cakes and pancakes, scones and biscuits were manageable, but without a built-in bread oven, the family had to rely on the village bakery to cook loaves, pies and cakes for them. If the house did have an oven built into the chimney, it was heated once a week by means of a fire of brushwood and sticks and when these had burnt down, the embers were spread flat to ensure an even heat. The oven retained its heat for 24 hours and first the bread was placed inside on a flat implement called a peel and then, when the warm loaves and rolls had been taken out, in went the cakes and pastries. As the century progressed, the kitchen range came into vogue and allowed the cook to prepare several different dishes all at the same time. Ranges were cleaner and more controllable than open fires, but

the fact that they were fuelled by coal made them expensive to run and meant that the stove and flues needed constant cleaning. The first gas stove was manufactured in 1825, but did not become popular until the 1880s, when more houses started to use gas for lighting, heating and cooking.

Meanwhile, the fashion for tea grew apace and by the 1870s, books of etiquette and household management were instructing ladies that 'Little Teas take place in the afternoon' – these very sociable occasions were also known as 'low tea', 'handed tea', 'kettledrums', 'at homes' and even 'tea fights'. In 1890, one fashion magazine informed readers that 'instead of five o'clock tea meetings, the custom, now, is to drop in any time between four and seven, when the kettle will be boiling … seven o'clock is on the verge of striking before the rooms are cleared, and then very often the hostess breathes a sigh of relief and hurries away to dress for a dinner party or the theatre.'

Our mode of dress these days is much more relaxed than in Victorian times and a stroll in the grounds of a National Trust property calls for sensible shoes and practical clothing (which in Britain usually means warm and weatherproof). But afternoon tea, for the upper-class lady of the late 19th century or Edwardian period, called for extreme elegance and femininity. Tight lacing was on the way out and loose, flowing tea gowns in chiffon, ninon, cashmere and lace allowed the wearer to indulge in afternoon tea in comfort while looking utterly charming. In 1890, a publication called *Beauty & Fashion* summed up the reasons for such garments: 'The first important item with a hostess in regard to afternoon tea is the selection of a becoming gown. The tea will taste sweeter, and the cups will look prettier, if she is robed in some gauze-like fabric of artistic make, and the dainty tea-gown is of just as much consequence to her as the beverage itself, and adds considerably to her good humour. If she knows that she is well-clad, and that the pretty flimsy lace and soft silk will bear the closest inspection of her particular friends, there is sure to be a charming air of satisfaction pervading her whole conversation, and her manner will be more than usually affable and gracious.' The fashion for tea gowns continued into the 20th century with fashion designers continuing to create 'tea jackets', 'afternoon-tea frocks' and 'hostess, tea and individual gowns' and in the 1930s, fashion houses were still advertising dresses that followed 'closely the latest trend of fashion and moderate in price'.

Going out for tea and cakes has been a favourite British pastime since 1875, when Stuart Cranston decided to place a few small tables and chairs in his tea retail store in Glasgow so that his customers could taste samples of his teas in comfort before deciding which to buy. Over the following 25 years, his sister Kate opened five new tearooms in the city, including the famous Willow Tea Rooms, which she commissioned Charles Rennie Mackintosh to design. Gradually new tearooms opened all over the country. Town dwellers got out their bicycles or clambered into carts and traps, climbed on board steam trains or walked to get out into the country where the air was clean and fresh, and cups of tea were available in cottage gardens and country tea rooms. Or picnic baskets were carefully packed with generous hunks of fruitcake and Bakewell tarts, Eccles cakes and apple pies, and families would find a quiet spot by the river or in the corner of a field where the children could romp and play with bats and balls while the grown-ups lazed under a shady tree. The first ten years or so of the 20th century saw the building of smart new hotels in London and these invariably included a palm court or elegant tea lounge where guests could take tea in the afternoon while a 'palm court orchestra' or string quartet played discreetly soothing music to suit the hushed elegance of the occasion.

And who was supplying all the tea that was being consumed around the country? Before 1834, the East India Company had the monopoly on the importation of tea from China into the London docks, but once that control was broken, other ports opened up to the tea trade and new companies were established in Bristol, Liverpool, Glasgow and elsewhere around the coast.

With the beginning of tea production in India and Ceylon, tea gradually became cheaper and more available and successful traders became very wealthy. An 1840 publication called *Tea and the Tea Trade* reported that tea consumption had gone up from 'a very few pounds till it has reached the astonishing extent of twenty-five millions per annum, and probably is capable of being carried still further. It may be literally said to have descended from the palace to the cottage, and from a fashionable and expensive luxury, has been converted into an essential comfort, if not an absolute necessity of life.' The book acknowledged that the retailing of tea had 'made some of our London bankers ... made some Members of Parliament ... enabled others to purchase landed estates'. One such successful trader was William Straw of Worksop, who set himself up in the town as a grocer and tea dealer in 1886. By 1920 he was doing so well that he could afford to buy an expensive villa at No 7 Blyth Grove, and the house was lived in by his family until 1990, when William Straw's son left it to the National Trust. And Julius Drew, another grocer who established the Home and Colonial Stores in 1878, made enough money to retire to Devon where he built the magnificent Castle Drogo – today also a Trust property – with the profits.

Tea was so popular then that companies didn't need to spend much of their revenue on advertising, but when they did publicise their teas, it was often based on its health benefits. The underlying message in many advertising slogans and images was that drinking tea led to a healthier and happier life. Lewis's department store in Birmingham praised their brand in an advertising poem as 'A tea beneficial, of beautiful blend; A tea mild and mellow that none can mend; A tea strong and savoury, lasting and luscious; A National tea, tea quite nutritious; A capital tea, choice too, and cheerful.' PG Tips emphasised their blend's digestive benefits, and because Typhoo wanted to be seen as a healthy drink, it was initially distributed through chemists' shops. Today, medical and scientific research has shown that the consumption of all types of tea – black, green, oolong, white and puerh – is beneficial to our health. The fact that people now recognise that tea can help the digestion, reduce cholesterol, reduce the risk of heart disease, help protect against certain cancers and protect our teeth from decay and the destructive effects of plaque has led to a growing interest in this wonderful drink.

CONVERSIONS

Weight	Liquid measure	Length	Temperature
15g (½oz)	15ml (½fl oz)	5mm (¼in)	110°C, 225°F, gas mark ¼
25g (1oz)	30ml (1fl oz)	1cm (½in)	120°C, 250°F, gas mark ½
40g (1½oz)	50ml (2fl oz)	1.5cm (⅝in)	140°C, 275°F, gas mark 1
55g (2oz)	75ml (2½fl oz)	2cm (¾in)	150°C, 300°F, gas mark 2
70g (2½oz)	100ml (3½fl oz)	2.5cm (1in)	160°C, 325°F, gas mark 3
85g (3oz)	125ml (4fl oz)	5cm (2in)	180°C, 350°F, gas mark 4
100g (3½oz)	150ml (5fl oz or ¼ pint)	7cm (2¾in)	190°C, 375°F, gas mark 5
115g (4oz)	200ml (7fl oz or ⅓ pint)	9cm (3½in)	200°C, 400°F, gas mark 6
125g (4½oz)	250ml (9fl oz)	10cm (4in)	220°C, 425°F, gas mark 7
140g (5oz)	300ml (10fl oz or ½ pint)	13cm (5in)	230°C, 450°F, gas mark 8
150g (5½oz)	350ml (12fl oz)	15cm (6in)	240°C, 475°F, gas mark 9
175g (6oz)	400ml (14fl oz)	18cm (7in)	
200g (7oz)	425ml (15fl oz or ¾ pint)	20cm (8in)	
225g (8oz)	500ml (18fl oz)	23cm (9in)	
250g (9oz)	600ml (20fl oz or 1 pint)	25cm (10in)	
300g (10½oz)		28cm (11in)	
350g (12oz)		30cm (12in)	
375g (13oz)			
400g (14oz)			
425g (15oz)			
450g (1lb)			
675g (1½lb)			
900g (2lb)			

AMERICAN EQUIVALENTS

Dry measures		
1 US cup	50g (¾oz)	breadcrumbs; cake crumbs
1 US cup	85g (3oz)	porridge or rolled oats
1 US cup	90g (3¼oz)	ground almonds; shredded coconut
1 US cup	100g (3½oz)	roughly chopped walnuts and other nuts; icing sugar; cocoa; drinking chocolate; flaked almonds; grated Cheddar cheese
1 US cup	150g (5½oz)	white flour; currants; rice flour; muesli; cornflour; chopped dates
1 US cup	175g (6oz)	wholemeal flour; oatmeal; raisins; sultanas; dried apricots; mixed candied peel
1 US cup	200g (7oz)	caster sugar; soft brown sugar; demerara sugar; rice; glacé cherries; semolina; chopped figs or plums
1 US cup	225g (8oz)	granulated sugar; curd cheese; cream cheese
1 US cup	300g (10½oz)	mincemeat; marmalade; jam
1 US cup	350g (12oz)	golden syrup; black treacle

Liquid measures		
⅛ US cup	30ml (1fl oz)	
¼ US cup	50ml (2fl oz)	
½ US cup	125ml (4fl oz)	
1 US cup	250ml (9fl oz)	
1¼ US cups	300ml (10fl oz)	
1¾ US cups	425ml (15fl oz)	
2 US cups	500ml (18fl oz)	
2½ US cups	600ml (20fl oz)	

Measures for fats		
¼ stick	25g (1oz)	
1 stick	100g (3½oz)	
(½ US cup)		

CAKES

Scones, muffins and fruited buns can be bought in supermarkets, but teatime cakes really are more exciting and satisfying when they are homemade. Thrill family and friends with scrummy chocolate cakes, fruit cakes packed full of tea-plumped vine fruits or locally grown apples and plums, or subtly flavoured with honey, saffron, spices, slivers of dried apricots and the wonderful texture of hazelnuts and almonds. Teatime wouldn't be teatime without such treats!

SUNDAY-BEST CHOCOLATE CAKE

A sumptuous cake for special occasions, the ingredients include two sorts of chocolate – cocoa powder and white chocolate. Cocoa powder is made by grinding down the seeds found inside cocoa pods into a thick creamy paste and then separating the cocoa butter from the cocoa solids. The cocoa solids can be dried into cocoa powder and the cocoa butter is used as the base for rich, smooth white chocolate.

FOR THE CAKE

225g (8oz) plain wholemeal
    flour, sifted
5 level teaspoons baking powder
225g (8oz) butter, softened
225g (8oz) light or dark soft
    brown sugar
5 large eggs, beaten
3 tablespoons cocoa powder,
    sifted

FOR THE FILLING AND
TOPPING

350ml (12fl oz) single cream
675g (24oz) white chocolate,
    grated
Grated dark chocolate, curls of
    white chocolate or chocolate
    buttons, to decorate

Makes 1 x 20cm (8in)
3-tier cake

Preheat the oven to 160°C, 325°F, gas mark 3. Grease and line three 20cm (8in) round sandwich tins. Place all the ingredients for the cake in a large bowl and beat thoroughly to give a soft dropping consistency (add a little water if too dry). Divide equally between the prepared tins and smooth the tops. Bake for about 30 minutes until the sponge springs back when lightly pressed. Remove from the oven and turn out on to a wire rack to cool. Next make the filling and topping. Bring the cream just to boiling point in a heavy pan and stir in the chocolate. Remove from the heat and stir until well blended. Leave in a cool place until it has achieved the right consistency for spreading. Use to sandwich the cakes together and to cover the top.

Decorate with grated dark chocolate, fat curls of white chocolate or chocolate buttons. This makes a spectacular gateau that is suitable for birthday parties or as a dinner-party dessert.

CHOCOLATE RUM CAKE

The flavours of chocolate and rum combine well together and this cake is a good example. Tea has a connection with rum since both were at one time smuggled into Britain together. Tea was so expensive that tea lovers found it difficult to afford a regular supply. So to provide cheaper tea, smugglers brought chests of tea (and bottles of rum, brandy, wines and other valuable items) from France and Holland where taxes were lower, and they distributed the goods through a very active and successful local black market.

FOR THE CAKE

250g (9oz) butter, softened
250g (9oz) caster sugar
4 eggs
250g (9oz) self-raising flour, sifted
100g (4oz) drinking chocolate powder
40g (1½oz) cocoa powder, sifted
A few drops of vanilla essence
2–3 tablespoons dark rum
150ml (5fl oz) milk

FOR THE FILLING AND ICING

500g (18oz) icing sugar, sifted
40g (1½oz) cocoa powder, sifted
225g (8oz) butter, softened
175g (6oz) caster sugar
2 tablespoons dark rum
65ml (2½fl oz) milk

Makes 1 x 20cm (8in)
round cake

Preheat the oven to 150°C, 300°F, gas mark 2. Grease and line a 20cm (8in) round tin. Beat together the butter and sugar until light and fluffy. Beat in the eggs, one at a time, beating hard after each addition. Combine the flour, drinking chocolate and cocoa and add to the mixture. Mix in carefully, taking care not to beat in any more air or the cake will flood over the top of the tin during cooking. Add the vanilla essence, rum and enough milk to mix to a soft dropping consistency. Turn into the prepared tin, smooth the top and hollow out the middle a little. Bake for 1½–1¾ hours until a skewer comes out clean. Remove from the oven and allow to cool in the tin for about 15 minutes before turning on to a wire rack to cool completely.

To make the icing and filling, beat all the ingredients together until light and fluffy. Cut the cake horizontally through the middle. Spread half the mixture on to the base and sandwich the other half of the cake on top. Spread the remaining filling on top of the cake and decorate with grated chocolate, half walnuts or by making a pattern with the prongs of a fork. This is an impressive, deep cake that looks and tastes delicious.

CHOCOLATE ORANGE DRIZZLE CAKE

Chocolate cakes like this one are wonderful accompanied by a strong, black tea such as Kenya or a strong Ceylon or Assam. Brew the tea for 4–5 minutes to make sure that all the flavour and goodness are drawn out into the boiling water. Stronger teas often drink well with a little milk so add a small quantity of semi-skimmed, which works best in tea.

FOR THE CAKE
175g (6oz) butter, softened
175g (6oz) caster sugar
3 large eggs
Grated rind of 2 oranges
175g (6oz) self-raising flour,
    sifted
2 tablespoons milk

FOR THE TOPPING
Juice of 2 oranges
100g (4oz) granulated sugar
50g (2oz) milk or plain
    chocolate

Makes 1 x 900g (2lb) loaf
or 18cm (7in) round cake

Preheat the oven to 180°C, 350°F, gas mark 4. Grease and line a 900g (2lb) loaf tin or an 18cm (7in) round tin. Cream together the butter and sugar until light and fluffy. Add the eggs, one at a time, and beat well. Add the grated orange rind, flour and milk and fold in with a metal spoon. Turn into the prepared tin, smooth the top and bake for 30–40 minutes until a skewer comes out clean. Remove from the oven and leave to cool in the tin. When cool, score the top of the cake lightly with a sharp knife. Put the orange juice and granulated sugar into a pan and heat gently until the sugar has dissolved. Bring to the boil and boil for 1–2 minutes. Pour over the cake. When all the juice has soaked in, carefully remove the cake from the tin. Melt the chocolate and pour over the top. Make a pattern with the prongs of a fork and leave to set.

Right: Chocolate Orange Drizzle Cake

LIGHT SPONGE CAKE

This is a recipe from Chirk Castle in Wales, where afternoon tea was a very elegant but small meal consisting of sandwiches the size of a postage stamp. Sometimes in cold weather a dish of hot buttered muffins or warm scones were also served. One footman who used to be responsible for taking tea into the salon once said, 'When clearing away the teas I always remember you had to eat at least four sandwiches to even taste them!'

200g (7oz) granulated or
   caster sugar
2 large or 3 medium eggs
150g (5oz) self-raising flour,
   sifted
a pinch of salt
1 teaspoon baking powder
100ml (4fl oz) milk
50g (2oz) butter
2–3 drops vanilla essence

Makes 1 x 20cm (8in)
round cake

Preheat the oven to 160°C, 325°F, gas mark 3. Grease and line a 20cm (8in) round tin. Beat together the sugar and eggs until thick and creamy. Add the flour, salt and baking powder and mix well. Put the milk in a small pan and heat gently. Melt the butter in the milk and bring to the boil. When boiling, add to the flour mixture with the vanilla essence and beat well to give a runny consistency. Turn into the prepared tin and bang the tin sharply on the table to remove air bubbles. Bake for 20–25 minutes until a skewer comes out clean. Remove from the oven and cool in the tin for 15 minutes before turning out on to a wire rack to cool completely.

   This cake is quick and easy to make, and is delicious served with fruit and cream. It is ideal for freezing.

Left: Light Sponge Cake

CHOCOLATE TRUFFLE CAKE

This is named after the soft, velvety smooth confectionery that originated in France. The ganache centre of a truffle is made of solid chocolate and cream and is often flavoured with vanilla, brandy or rum. The name probably comes from the similarity in appearance between a chocolate truffle and the small, dark fungus so highly prized in France. This chocolate treat does not require cooking.

675g (1½lb) left-over cake (any sort), broken into small pieces
100g (4oz) jam (any sort)
50g (2oz) mixed, unsalted nuts, roughly chopped
50g (2oz) cocoa powder, sifted
3–4 tablespoons orange juice
225–275g (8–10oz) milk or plain chocolate
50g (2oz) blanched, split almonds, toasted

Makes 9 pieces

Grease and line an 18cm (7in) square tin. Mix together the cake, jam, nuts, cocoa powder and enough orange juice to bind the mixture. Press into the prepared tin and smooth the top. Melt the chocolate and pour over the surface. Spread evenly and sprinkle with the almonds. Place in the refrigerator to set. When set, cut into pieces and lift carefully out of the tin.

This is an excellent and quick way to turn left-over cake into a rich, delicious chocolate treat.

CAROB CRUNCH

For anyone who cannot eat chocolate, carob is an ideal alternative and is available in health-food shops. This recipe comes from Cliveden in Berkshire, in the grounds of which is a small octagonal temple which serves as a tea house. On large estates like this, a whole day was sometimes set aside for an excursion to one of the follies, temples, pavilions and grottoes in the grounds. The assembly made their way to the rendezvous, indulged in a leisurely lunch or afternoon tea and then returned to the house.

225g (8oz) butter
25g (1oz) carob powder
225g (8oz) plain wholemeal
   flour, sifted
150g (5oz) light or dark soft
   brown sugar
100g (4oz) shredded coconut

Makes 12 pieces

Preheat the oven to 190°C, 375°F, gas mark 5. Grease an 18 x 28cm (7 x 11in) Swiss roll tin. In a medium-sized pan, melt the butter and add the carob powder. Stir over a gentle heat until the carob is dissolved. Add the flour, sugar and coconut and mix well. Turn into the prepared tin and press well down. Smooth the top and bake for 20–25 minutes until firm. Remove from the oven and leave to cool in the tin. When cold, cut into pieces and lift from the tin.

TOFFEE BARS

What could be more fun than going out to tea at one of the National Trust tearooms and enjoying something sweet and sticky like these cakes? The idea of tearooms started in Glasgow and spread to London when a well-known bread company called the ABC (the Aerated Bread Company) decided to turn a spare back room at their London Bridge branch into a public tearoom. Their success prompted other companies to open their own tearooms, and soon all of Britain was enjoying 'going out to tea'.

FOR THE CAKE
100g (4oz) butter, softened
100g (4oz) light soft brown
    sugar
1 egg yolk
50g (2oz) plain flour, sifted
50g (2oz) porridge oats

FOR THE TOPPING
75g (3oz) plain chocolate
25g (1oz) butter
50g (2oz) walnuts or almonds,
    chopped

Makes 12 bars

Preheat the oven to 190°C, 375°F, gas mark 5. Grease an 18 x 28cm (7 x 11in) Swiss roll tin. Beat together the butter, sugar and egg yolk until light and smooth. Add the flour and oats and mix well. Press into the prepared tin and bake for 15–20 minutes until lightly browned. Remove from the oven and leave to cool slightly in the tin. Melt together the chocolate and butter for the topping and spread over the cake. Cover with the chopped nuts and leave to set. While still warm, cut into bars and leave in the tin until completely cold.

MADEIRA CAKE

This simple sponge cake was traditionally served with a glass of Madeira wine but today it makes an excellent accompaniment to a cup of Ceylon or Darjeeling tea, or for a change, perhaps a China oolong or Keemun. It needs to be eaten very fresh when it is soft and light.

225g (8oz) plain flour, sifted
1 teaspoon baking powder
175g (6oz) butter, softened
175g (6oz) caster sugar
Grated rind of half a lemon
3 eggs
2 tablespoons milk

Makes 1 x 7in (18cm)
round cake

Preheat the oven to 180°C, 350°F, gas mark 4. Grease and line an 18cm (7in) round tin. Mix together the flour and baking powder. Beat together the butter, sugar and lemon rind until light and fluffy. Beat in the eggs, one at a time, adding 2 tablespoons of the flour and baking powder mix with the last two. Fold in the remaining flour, then gently mix in the milk. Turn into the prepared tin and bake for 1 hour until a skewer comes out clean. Remove from the oven and turn out on to a wire rack to cool.

17th-CENTURY HONEY CAKE

It is thought that a daily dose of honey helps to boost the body's supply of beneficial antioxidants that protect us against age-related diseases. Tea is also a source of antioxidants and offers protection against certain cancers and heart disease. So a slice of this honey cake with two or three cups of tea will not just taste good — it will do you good as well.

FOR THE CAKE
175g (6oz) butter, softened
175g (6oz) caster sugar
3 eggs, beaten
175g (6oz) white or wholemeal
    self-raising four, sifted
1 teaspoon baking powder
1 tablespoon clear honey
A few drops of almond essence

FOR THE TOPPING
1 dessertspoon clear honey
Juice of 1 lemon

FOR THE ICING
150g (5oz) cream cheese
Juice of half a lemon
175g (6oz) icing sugar, sifted

Makes 1 x 900g (2lb) loaf or
18cm (7in) round cake

Preheat the oven to 180°C, 350°F, gas mark 4. Grease and line a 900g (2lb) loaf tin or an 18cm (7in) round tin. Beat together the butter and sugar until light and fluffy. Add the eggs, flour and baking powder and beat hard. Add the honey and almond essence and continue beating for 1–2 minutes. Turn into the prepared tin and bake for 1–1¼ hours, until a skewer comes out clean. (After half an hour, cover the top with a double layer of greaseproof paper as the cake tends to darken quite quickly.) Remove from the oven. Mix together the honey and lemon juice for the topping and pour over the top. Leave to cool in the tin, then turn out. Beat together the cream cheese, lemon juice and icing sugar and spread over the cooled cake. Make a pattern with the prongs of a fork and serve.

DOROTHY WORDSWORTH'S FAVOURITE CAKE

Caraway seed comes from a herb related to the parsley family and since medieval times has been used in breads, cakes and cheeses. Seed cakes were very popular in Victorian times, when cookery books always included at least one recipe. The seed is thought to aid digestion.

175g (6oz) butter, softened
175g (6oz) caster sugar
3 eggs
3 teaspoons caraway seeds
225g (8oz) plain flour, sifted
1 teaspoon baking powder
Pinch of salt
1 tablespoon ground almonds
1 tablespoon milk

Makes 1 x 900g (2lb) loaf

Preheat the oven to 180°C, 350°F, gas mark 4. Grease and line a 900g (2lb) loaf tin. Beat together the butter and sugar until light and fluffy, then beat in the eggs. Add the caraway seeds, flour, baking powder, salt, almonds and milk and mix carefully so that all the ingredients are evenly distributed. Turn into the prepared tin and bake for 45–55 minutes until a skewer comes out clean. Remove from the oven and leave to cool in the tin.

FEATHERLIGHT WHOLEWHEAT CAKE

Using the correct measures when baking is obviously very important and it is equally important to use the correct measure when brewing tea. The best guideline is to allow 2.5–3g to 200ml of water. Different teas brew at different rates, so use a timer to be sure not to spoil the tea. Small-leafed tea takes approximately 2–3 minutes to brew. Large-leafed tea needs 4–5 minutes.

FOR THE CAKE

100g (4oz) butter, softened

100g (4oz) light or dark soft
   brown sugar

2 eggs, separated

1 tablespoon cold water

100g (4oz) wholewheat self-
   raising flour, sifted

FOR THE FILLING AND ICING

200g (7oz) low-fat cream cheese

50g (2oz) icing sugar, sifted

75g (3oz) walnuts, chopped

TO DECORATE

9 half walnuts

Makes 1 x 18cm (7in)
round cake

Preheat the oven to 180°C, 350°F, gas mark 4. Grease two 18cm (7in) round sandwich tins. Beat together the butter and sugar until light and fluffy. Beat together the egg yolks and water, add to the mixture and beat hard. Fold in the flour. Whisk the egg whites until stiff, then fold in. Turn into the prepared tins and smooth. Bake for 20–25 minutes until well risen and golden. Remove from the oven and leave to cool in the tins for 5 minutes, then turn out on to a wire rack to cool completely. Meanwhile beat together the ingredients for the filling until light and fluffy. When the cake is cold, spread half of the mixture on one cake and place the other cake on top. Ice with the remaining mixture and decorate with half walnuts.

THRESHING CAKE

Threshing time was the most important time of the farming calendar, when the grain was gathered in and stored for use during the winter. The 15 to 20 extra workers had to be fed and this cake helped to satisfy their hunger during the afternoon break. Many areas of Britain had their own dishes for threshing time, and this fruit loaf was a Welsh speciality.

100g (4oz) dripping or lard
225g (8oz) plain flour, sifted
100g (4oz) caster sugar
225g (8oz) mixed dried fruit
1 egg, beaten
¼ teaspoon bicarbonate of soda
   dissolved in 1 tablespoon
   buttermilk or sour milk
A little extra buttermilk
   or sour milk

Makes 1 x 900g (2lb) loaf

Preheat the oven to 190°C, 375°F, gas mark 5. Grease and line a 900g (2lb) loaf tin. Rub the fat into the flour. Add the sugar and dried fruit and stir well. Add the beaten egg and bicarbonate of soda and mix with enough buttermilk or sour milk to give a soft consistency. Turn into the prepared tin and bake for 1½ hours until a skewer comes out clean. Remove from the oven and turn on to a wire rack to cool.

PLUM LOAF

Unusually, this cake uses fresh plums, which give a slightly tart flavour and juicy texture to the dough. Plums appear to have been grown in England since the 15th century and traditional plum-growing areas are in the vale of Evesham in Worcestershire, parts of Warwickshire and East Anglia. In Cornwall, the bitter-flavoured Kea plum grows on the Fal estuary.

225g (8oz) fresh plums, stoned
(weighed after stoning)
100g (4oz) butter, softened
50g (2oz) light soft brown sugar
2 tablespoons golden syrup
2 eggs
225g (8oz) self-raising flour,
sifted
2 teaspoons mixed spice
A little milk
Caster sugar for dusting

Makes 1 x 900g (2lb) loaf

Preheat the oven to 180°C, 350°F, gas mark 4. Grease and line a 900g (2lb) loaf tin. Chop the plums coarsely. Beat together the butter, sugar and syrup until light and fluffy. Add the eggs one at a time with a little flour, beating hard after each addition. Fold in the remaining flour, the spice and plums and enough milk to mix to a soft dropping consistency. Turn into the prepared tin and bake for 1¼ hours until a skewer comes out clean. Remove from the oven and turn out on to a wire rack to cool. Before serving, dust with caster sugar.

This is an unusual cake and an excellent way to use spare fresh plums. The fruit gives the loaf a soft, moist texture and the spicy flavour complements the taste of the plums. Eat freshly baked, as the cake tends to dry out if left.

KENTISH HOP PICKERS' CAKE

In the 17th and 18th centuries, up to 80,000 itinerant harvest workers arrived in Kent each September to gather the hops for beer-making. Whole families would travel down from the East End of London and needed feeding by the hop farmers, and this modern recipe was developed from the cakes baked by the farmers' wives for teatime in the hop gardens.

275g (10oz) self-raising flour, sifted
1 teaspoon ground ginger
1 teaspoon mixed spice
175g (6oz) butter, softened
100g (4oz) light soft brown sugar
100g (4oz) sultanas
100g (4oz) currants
50g (2oz) mixed candied peel
400ml (15fl oz) milk
1 tablespoon black treacle
½ teaspoon bicarbonate of soda
1 teaspoon cream of tartar

Makes 1 x 900g (2lb) loaf

Preheat the oven to 160°C, 325°F, gas mark 3. Grease and line a 900g (2lb) loaf tin. Mix together the flour, ginger and spice and rub in the butter. Add the sugar, dried fruit and peel and mix well. Warm the milk and treacle together and add the bicarbonate of soda and cream of tartar. Gradually add to the flour mixture and beat well. Pour into the prepared tin and bake for 1½ hours until a skewer comes out clean. Remove from the oven and turn out on to a wire rack to cool.

OLD PECULIER FRUIT CAKE

Old Peculier beer is brewed by Theakstons, founded in Yorkshire in 1827. Its rich, dark, smooth character adds the subtle, sweet flavour of hops to this fruit cake, making it really distinctive.

100g (4oz) butter, softened
50g (2oz) light soft brown sugar
50g (2oz) caster sugar
2 eggs
75g (3oz) plain flour, sifted
75g (3oz) self-raising flour, sifted
100g (4oz) currants
50g (2oz) raisins
50g (2oz) sultanas
Juice and grated rind of 1 lemon
70ml (2¾fl oz) Theakston's Old
    Peculier ale

Makes 1 x 900g (2lb) loaf

Grease and line a 900g (2lb) loaf tin. Beat together the butter and sugars until light and fluffy. Add the eggs one at a time and beat well. Fold in the flour, dried fruit and lemon juice and rind. Add the Old Peculier and stir well. Turn into the prepared tin, cover and leave to stand overnight. The next day, preheat the oven to 150°C, 300°F, gas mark 2. Bake the cake for 1¾–2 hours until a skewer comes out clean. Remove from the oven and turn out on to a wire rack to cool.

BOILED WHISKEY CAKE

For festive occasions, the Irish added all the usual spices, butter and dried fruits to their plainer, everyday bread and cake mixtures to make them a little more special, and they also included one more, very Irish ingredient – whiskey! This recipe comes from Castle Ward in County Down where the wife of the 6th Viscount Bangor made a habit of serving afternoon tea to a number of guests in her sitting room. She used a willow-pattern tea service, whose decoration is based on a Chinese tale of love and family intrigue.

275g (10oz) raisins and currants
225ml (8fl oz) water
225g (8oz) light or dark soft
    brown sugar
100g (4oz) butter
225g (8oz) plain flour, sifted
2 teaspoons mixed spice
1½ teaspoons bicarbonate
    of soda
1½ teaspoons ground ginger
2 large eggs, beaten
50ml (2fl oz) Irish whiskey

Makes 1 x 900g (2lb) loaf

Preheat the oven to 160°C, 325°F, gas mark 3. Grease and line a 900g (2lb) loaf tin. Put the mixed fruit, water, sugar and butter into a pan and bring to the boil, stirring occasionally. Leave to cool for a few minutes. Add a little of the flour, the mixed spice, bicarbonate of soda and ginger, then mix and leave to stand until cool. Add the beaten eggs, the whiskey and the remaining flour, mix well and turn into the prepared tin. Bake for 1½–1¾ hours until a skewer comes out clean. Remove from the oven and turn out on to a wire rack to cool.

GIANT'S BOILED FRUIT CAKE

The Irish drink more tea than any other nation in the world, Britain and the Arab states coming next in the list of great tea consumers. The strong black tea that they like to drink with milk and sugar is excellent with a slice of this fruit cake from Giant's Causeway.

175g (6oz) butter, softened
175g (6oz) granulated or
    caster sugar
300ml (10fl oz) water
100g (4oz) raisins
100g (4oz) sultanas
100g (4oz) currants
50g (2oz) glacé cherries, halved
225g (8oz) plain flour, sifted
2 teaspoons mixed spice
1 teaspoon baking powder
1 teaspoon ground ginger
50g (2oz) walnuts,
    roughly chopped
2 large eggs, beaten

Makes 1 x 900g (2lb) loaf

Put the butter, sugar, water, dried fruit and glacé cherries into a pan. Bring to the boil and simmer for 10 minutes. Remove from the heat and leave to stand overnight. The next day preheat the oven to 180°C, 350°F, gas mark 4. Grease and line a 900g (2lb) loaf tin. Mix together the dry ingredients and walnuts and add to the boiled mixture with the beaten eggs. Mix thoroughly and turn into the prepared tin. Bake for 1–1½ hours until a skewer comes out clean. Remove from the oven and leave to cool in the tin for about 15 minutes before turning out on to a wire rack to cool completely.

BANBURY CAKES

Banbury cakes date back to pagan days and are thought to have been eaten at May Day celebrations. Recipes have changed greatly over the centuries, varying from a type of fruited bread flavoured with caraway seeds, to pastry cases filled with fruit, saffron and sherry. Today's cakes are a fruit-filled pastry with a flaky outer case and plump dried fruit inside.

350g (12oz) puff pastry (see page 90)
50g (2oz) butter
100g (4oz) currants
50g (2oz) mixed candied peel
¼ teaspoon ground cinnamon
½ teaspoon allspice or grated nutmeg
25g (1oz) light or dark soft brown sugar
1 tablespoon dark rum
A little milk or water
1 egg white, lightly beaten
Caster sugar for dusting

Makes 11–12 cakes

Make the pastry according to the instructions on page 90 and chill for at least 30 minutes. Melt the butter in a small pan and add the dried fruit, peel, spices, brown sugar and rum. Stir and leave to cool. Preheat the oven to 230°C, 450°F, gas mark 8. Grease two baking trays. On a lightly floured board, roll out the pastry to a thickness of 0.5cm (¼in) and cut into rounds approximately 10cm (4in) in diameter. Place a spoonful of the fruit mixture on each circle, dampen the edges of the pastry with a little milk or water and gather the edges together. Seal well, turn each cake over and roll gently to a neat oval shape. Cut three slashes in the top and place on the prepared trays. Brush the tops with the beaten egg white and dust with caster sugar. Bake for 10–15 minutes until golden. Remove from the oven and lift on to a wire rack to cool slightly before serving.

CORNISH BLACK CAKE

Typical of recipes from this part of England, Cornish Black Cake uses several different spices and plenty of dried fruits, all of which would, in the past, have been brought into the country through the Cornish ports. Some recipes include dark molasses sugar to give an even richer colour to the mixture.

175g (6oz) butter, softened
175g (6oz) caster sugar
3–4 eggs, beaten
100g (4oz) plain flour, sifted
100g (4oz) ground rice
½ teaspoon mixed spice
½ teaspoon grated nutmeg
½ teaspoon ground cinnamon
½ teaspoon baking powder
½ teaspoon bicarbonate of soda
450g (1lb) currants
100g (4oz) mixed candied peel
50g (2oz) sultanas
50g (2oz) raisins
75g (3oz) almonds, blanched and
    chopped
1 tablespoon brandy
A little milk for mixing

Makes 1 x 20cm (8in)
round cake

Preheat the oven to 170°C, 325°F, gas mark 3. Grease and line a 20cm (8in) round tin. Beat together the butter and sugar until light and fluffy. Add the eggs, flour, ground rice, spices, baking powder, bicarbonate of soda, dried fruit, peel, almonds and brandy and mix carefully until all the ingredients are evenly distributed. If necessary add a little milk to give a soft mixture. Turn into the prepared tin, smooth the top and bake for 1 hour. Reduce the oven temperature to 140°C, 275°F, gas mark 1 and cook for a further 1–1½ hours until a skewer comes out clean.

Remove from the oven and leave to cool in the tin for 15 minutes, then turn out on to a wire rack to cool completely.

Right: Cornish Black Cake.
Next page: Banbury Cakes.

ALMOND-TOPPED APRICOT CAKE

This really delicious cake is made to a recipe from Petworth House in West Sussex, which has an impressive collection of tea porcelain. The word 'china' entered the English language in the 17th century when porcelain first arrived from China. Dishes, plates, bowls and saucers were described as cheyney, chenea, chiney or cheny and, since the European potters only knew how to make tableware from earthenware or stoneware, these Oriental wares were much sought after.

FOR THE CAKE
175g (6oz) butter, softened
175g (6oz) caster sugar
3 eggs
175g (6oz) self-raising flour, sifted
75g (3oz) ground almonds
100g (4oz) ready-to-use dried apricots, chopped

FOR THE TOPPING
50g (2oz) butter
50g (2oz) demerara sugar
1 tablespoon golden syrup
50g (2oz) flaked almonds

Makes 1 x 23cm (9in) round cake

Preheat the oven to 180°C, 350°F, gas mark 4. Grease and line the base of a 23cm (9in) loose-bottomed round tin. Beat together the butter and sugar until light and fluffy. Beat in the eggs one at a time, adding a tablespoon of flour with each. Fold in the remaining flour, the ground almonds and the apricots and mix well. Turn into the prepared tin and bake for 40 minutes. Meanwhile prepare the topping. In a small pan mix together the butter, sugar and syrup and heat gently until the sugar dissolves. Remove from the heat and stir in the almonds. When the 40 minutes' cooking time is up, remove the cake from the oven and spoon the topping over the top. Return to the oven and bake for a further 10–15 minutes until golden brown. Remove from the oven and leave to cool in the tin.

Left: Almond-topped Apricot Cake.
Previous page: Simnel Cake.

SIMNEL CAKE

Simnel cakes were originally made for Mothering Sunday, the fourth Sunday in Lent, when children working away from home would return to their families in order to worship at the mother church. They would bring a cake as a gift for their mother, often made by their employer's wife. The eleven balls of marzipan represent the eleven apostles without Judas.

550g (1lb 4oz) marzipan
175g (6oz) butter, softened
150g (5oz) light soft brown
  sugar
3 eggs, beaten
15g (½oz) glycerine
15g (½oz) glucose
100g (4oz) strong plain
  white flour
50g (2oz) ordinary plain
  white flour
25g (1oz) ground almonds
1 teaspoon mixed spice
½ teaspoon grated nutmeg
350g (12oz) sultanas
250g (9oz) currants
100g (4oz) mixed candied peel
A little apricot jam for fixing the
  marzipan topping in place

Makes 1 x 20cm (8in)
round cake

Preheat the oven to 180°C, 350°F, gas mark 4. Grease a 20cm (8in) round tin, line with a double layer of greaseproof paper and grease well. Divide the marzipan into three portions, one slightly smaller than the others. On a sugared board, roll out one of the two equal portions to a circle just smaller than the diameter of the tin. Beat together the butter and sugar until light and fluffy. Add the beaten eggs, glycerine and glucose and beat again. Mix together the flour, almonds and spices and gradually add to the mixture, stirring gently to blend. Do not beat. Add the dried fruit and peel and fold gently in. Turn half the mixture into the prepared tin and smooth the top. Place the circle of marzipan on top and then cover with the remaining cake mixture. Smooth the top and bake for 1 hour (if the top starts to become too brown, cover with a double layer of greaseproof paper), then reduce the oven temperature to 160°C, 325°F, gas mark 3 and bake for a further 45 minutes to 1 hour until a skewer comes out clean. Remove from the oven and leave to cool in the tin for 15 minutes before turning out on to a wire rack to cool completely. When cold, brush the top with apricot jam. Roll out the second marzipan portion to make a circle to fit the top of the cake. Put it in place and press gently. Form the remaining marzipan into eleven small balls and arrange them around the rim of the cake, sticking them on with apricot jam. Turn the grill to a moderate heat and place the cake underneath for a few minutes until the marzipan just begins to brown.

WHOLEMEAL CIDER CAKE

Devonshire apples have been used to make cider since the 13th century, and in the 17th century the orchards were extended with the sole purpose of manufacturing more cider. Use some to soak dried fruit before mixing into a fruit cake and it adds an extra zing to the final flavour.

100g (4oz) sultanas
75g (3oz) currants
25g (1oz) mixed candied peel
150ml (5fl oz) cider
150g (5oz) self-raising
    wholemeal flour, sifted
75g (3oz) dark soft brown sugar
50g (2oz) hazelnuts or blanched
    almonds, chopped
Finely grated rind of 1 lemon
Finely grated rind of 1 orange
1 eating apple, peeled,
    cored and chopped
2 medium eggs, beaten

Makes 1 x 900g (2lb) loaf

Put the dried fruit, peel and the cider into a pan and bring to the boil. Remove from the heat and leave to stand overnight. The following day preheat the oven to 180°C, 350°F, gas mark 4. Grease and line a 900g (2lb) loaf tin. Mix together the flour, sugar, nuts, orange and lemon rind, apple and beaten eggs and pour in the cider mixture. Beat thoroughly, then turn into the prepared tin. Bake for about 1 hour until a skewer comes out clean. Remove from the oven and turn out on to a wire rack to cool.

SPICE CAKE

This is made to a recipe from Clandon Park in Surrey, a Georgian country house that has a strong link to Catherine of Braganza, the Portuguese princess who married Charles II in 1662 and is responsible for introducing tea to the English court. Portugal and Holland were the first European countries to start trading with China and brought home cargoes of tea, which were re-exported to other European cities including London.

450g (1lb) plain flour, sifted
4 teaspoons mixed spice
A pinch of salt
225g (8oz) Trex or similar white
    shortening, softened
175g (6oz) caster sugar
175g (6oz) sultanas
175g (6oz) currants
300ml (10fl oz) milk
2 teaspoons white wine vinegar
2 teaspoons bicarbonate of soda
2 tablespoons demerara sugar
    for sprinkling

Makes 1 x 20cm (8in)
square cake

Preheat the oven to 160°C, 325°F, gas mark 3. Grease and line a 20cm (8in) square tin. Mix together the flour, spice and salt and rub in the fat. Add the caster sugar and dried fruit and mix well. Mix together the milk, vinegar and bicarbonate of soda and add to the mixture. Mix to a soft, fairly wet dough and turn into the prepared tin. Smooth the top and sprinkle with the demerara sugar. Bake for 1–1¼ hours until a skewer comes out clean. Remove from the oven and leave to cool in the tin.

BOODLE CAKE

The quirky name of this cake may come from Boodles Club, which was founded in 1752 in St James's Street, London, and gave its name to a popular orange fool. Or it may derive from an old noun meaning a delight, dessert, feast, luxury, titbit or treat! This recipe comes from Polesden Lacey, where plenty of boodles were enjoyed at the afternoon teas hosted by Mrs Ronald Greville over the first few decades of the 20th century.

275g (10oz) butter, softened
450g (1lb) plain flour, sifted
275g (10oz) light soft brown or
   raw cane sugar
450g (1lb) raisins
2 eggs, beaten
300ml (10fl oz) milk

Makes 1 x 23cm (9in)
square cake

Preheat the oven to 160°C, 325°F, gas mark 3. Grease and line a 23cm (9in) square tin. Rub the butter into the flour until the mixture resembles breadcrumbs. Stir in the sugar and raisins. Add the eggs and milk and mix to a soft dough. Turn into the prepared tin, spread out evenly with a palette knife and bake for 2 hours until a skewer comes out clean. Remove from the oven and turn out on to a wire rack to cool.

MINCEMEAT CAKE

Mincemeat really was once minced meat mixed up with spices, dried fruit, lemon peel, grated apple and brandy or rum. In most modern mincemeats, the only remaining part of the meat is suet, although vegetarian varieties replace this with butter. If eating a strongly spiced cake or pastry like this at teatime, choose a tea like China black Keemun or Yunnan, a Nilgiri from southern India or a strong English Breakfast blend.

225g (8oz) self-raising flour, sifted
150g (5oz) butter, softened
150g (5oz) light or dark soft brown sugar
75g (3oz) sultanas
450g (1lb) mincemeat
2 eggs, beaten
25–50g (1–2oz) flaked almonds

Makes 1 x 20cm (8in) round cake

Preheat the oven to 160°C, 325°F, gas mark 3. Grease and line a 20cm (8in) round tin. Keeping aside the flaked almonds, put all the ingredients into a bowl and mix thoroughly. Turn into the prepared tin and sprinkle the flaked almonds over the top. Bake for 1¾ hours until a skewer comes out clean. Remove from the oven and leave in the tin for about 15 minutes before turning out on to a wire rack to cool completely.

SIMONE SEKERS'S FRUIT PARKIN

Parkin is gingerbread made with oatmeal instead of flour and has a lovely nutty texture. Parkins are traditionally a Hallowe'en speciality and probably derive from the pagan practice of baking oatmeal and spice cakes for celebrations marking the beginning of winter. In Derbyshire, they were named after Thor, the Scandinavian god of thunder, war and agriculture. The cakes were also sometimes referred to as 'tharve' cakes (the hearth cakes) since they were cooked on a bakestone on an open kitchen fire.

400ml (15fl oz) water
100g (4oz) lard
175g (6oz) light or dark
   soft brown sugar
225g (8oz) golden syrup
225g (8oz) black treacle
100g (4oz) currants
50g (2oz) mixed candied peel
450g (1lb) plain flour, sifted
225g (8oz) medium oatmeal
2 teaspoons mixed spice
1½ teaspoons ground ginger
Pinch of salt and 1 teaspoon
   bicarbonate of soda dissolved
   in a little water

Makes 24 slices

Preheat the oven to 160°C, 325°F, gas mark 3. Grease and line a deep roasting tin measuring approximately 20 x 30cm (8 x 12in). Warm together the water, lard, sugar, syrup and treacle until melted. When cool, add all the other ingredients and mix thoroughly so that all are evenly distributed. Turn into the prepared tin and bake for 1–1½ hours until firm and well risen. Remove from the oven and leave to cool in the tin. When cold, cut into squares or slices.

18th-CENTURY PEPPER CAKE

Although generally used in savoury dishes, black pepper is sometimes added to cakes with ginger and other spices. Some recipes for this traditional Westmorland fruit cake also add dates and walnuts, but this one, from Wordsworth House in the Lake District, uses cloves, currants, raisins and peel.

450g (1lb) plain flour, sifted
1 teaspoon baking powder
100g (4oz) butter, softened
225g (8oz) caster sugar
100g (4oz) currants
100g (4oz) raisins
25g (1oz) mixed candied peel
½ teaspoon ground cloves
½ teaspoon ground ginger
½ teaspoon ground
   black pepper
225g (8oz) black treacle
2 eggs, beaten

Makes 1 x 23cm (9in)
round cake

Preheat the oven to 150°C, 300°F, gas mark 2. Grease and line a 23cm (9in) round deep cake tin. Mix together the flour and baking powder and rub in the butter until the mixture resembles fine breadcrumbs. Add all the other ingredients and mix to a thick batter. Turn into the prepared tin and bake for 2–2½ hours until a skewer comes out clean. Remove from the oven and leave to cool in the tin for 15 minutes before turning out on to a wire rack to cool completely. When cool, wrap in foil or clingfilm and store for a few days before using.

   The cake may be coated with marzipan and iced with a plain white icing made with 175–225g (6–8oz) icing sugar, sifted and mixed with 1–2 tablespoons cold water or lemon juice.

WELSH HONEY AND GINGER CAKE

In Wales, tea was always a very popular meal on Sundays and special occasions. Most Welsh homes used to rely on a bakestone for making bread, but a makeshift oven could be made by upturning a large iron cooking pot over the bakestone. In some homes, a baking oven was built into the fireplace so that cakes like this could be cooked ready for tea.

100g (4oz) butter
225g (8oz) clear honey
150ml (5fl oz) milk
450g (1lb) plain flour, sifted
Pinch of salt
2½ teaspoons baking powder
3 teaspoons ground ginger
100g (4oz) sultanas
50g (2oz) mixed candied peel
2 eggs, beaten

Makes 1 x 20cm (8in)
round cake

Preheat the oven to 180°C, 350°F, gas mark 4. Grease and line a 20cm (8in) round tin. Melt the butter gently with the honey and milk. Remove from the heat and leave to cool. Mix together the flour, salt, baking powder, ginger, dried fruit and peel. Add the beaten eggs and the butter mixture and mix to a soft consistency. Turn into the prepared tin and bake for 1¼–1½ hours until a skewer comes out clean. (Check the top after half an hour and, if it is beginning to brown too much, cover with a double layer of greaseproof paper.) Remove from the oven and turn out on to a wire rack to cool.

WELSH LARDY CAKE

Lardy cake was made to use up some of the fat left over from the family pig after the annual slaughter. Most rural families kept at least one pig, fattening it up on all the waste food during the year and then killing it in the autumn to provide food during the winter. Nothing was wasted – bacon, ham, fresh and salt pork provided joints of meat, the head was boiled to make a strong jelly stock, dripping was spread on bread and toast, and the lard was used for frying and for making pastry, puddings and lardy cakes.

15g (½oz) fresh yeast (to substitute dried yeast, see page 85)
1 tablespoon caster sugar
300ml (10fl oz) warm water
450g (1lb) plain flour, sifted
1 teaspoon salt
225g (8oz) lard, softened
100g (4oz) currants
50g (2oz) mixed candied peel
50g (2oz) caster or granulated sugar
A little extra plain flour

Makes 9 generous pieces

Cream together the yeast and caster sugar and mix with the warm water. Mix together the flour and salt, add the yeast mixture and mix to a soft dough. Knead for 3–4 minutes, then put in a bowl and leave in a warm place for 1–1½ hours until doubled in size. Preheat the oven to 200°C, 400°F, gas mark 6. Grease a 23cm (9in) square tin. On a floured board, roll out the dough to a thickness of 1cm (½in). Divide the lard, currants, peel and sugar into four equal portions. Spread a quarter of the lard on the dough and sprinkle over a quarter of the currants, peel and sugar and a little flour. Fold the dough in half and repeat the rolling, dotting and folding process three more times until all the ingredients are used. Place the folded dough in the prepared tin and bake for 25–30 minutes until golden brown. Remove from the oven and leave to cool in the tin. When cold, cut into squares and lift out of the tin. To serve, warm gently in the oven or microwave.

FLORENTINE SLICE

This rich chocolate slice is made to a recipe from Kingston Lacy in Dorset, once the home of the Bankes family. Margaret Bankes, who lived there in the 17th and 18th centuries, began buying teaware for the house and between 1701 and 1710, she acquired various 'setts of tea dishes and saucers', 'a kenester', a china sugar dish, a pair of tea tongs and 10 teapots. She also purchased 'a black Japan table for my closet' (where she took tea) and four more tea tables. This rich, gooey cake contains no flour, so is ideal for people who cannot eat wheat.

350g (12oz) good-quality milk or
   plain chocolate
350g (12oz) mixed dried fruit
   (raisins, sultanas, currants,
   candied peel)
100g (4oz) glacé cherries
100g (4oz) shredded coconut
100g (4oz) caster sugar
50g (2oz) butter, melted
2 eggs, beaten

Makes 16 slices

Line a 20 x 28cm (8 x 11in) tin with foil. Melt the chocolate and spread evenly in the base of the tin. Leave to cool in the refrigerator until set. Preheat the oven to 180°C, 350°F, gas mark 4. Mix together the dried fruit, glacé cherries, coconut, sugar, butter and beaten eggs and spread evenly over the chocolate. Bake for 25 minutes until golden brown. Remove from the oven and leave to cool in the tin. When cool, place the tin in the refrigerator until really cold. Cut into fingers and turn out of the tin.

TRADITIONAL CHRISTMAS CAKE

Our traditional Christmas cakes evolved from the winter gruel eaten by pagans to celebrate the winter solstice.
Spices and dried fruits were later added to enrich the festive porridge.

FOR THE CAKE
225g (8oz) currants
225g (8oz) sultanas
225g (8oz) raisins
100g (4oz) glacé cherries,
    chopped
½ glass brandy and port, mixed
1 teaspoon vanilla essence
1 teaspoon almond essence
225g (8oz) butter, softened
225g (8oz) soft brown sugar
4 large eggs, separated
225g (8oz) self-raising flour,
    sifted
1 teaspoon baking powder
1 teaspoon mixed spice

Makes 1 x 20cm (8in)
square cake or 1 x 23cm (9in)
round cake

Place the dried fruit, cherries, brandy and port, vanilla essence and
almond essence in a bowl and leave to soak overnight. The next day,
preheat the oven to 150°C, 300°F, gas mark 2. Grease and line a
20cm (8in) square tin or a 23cm (9in) round tin. Beat together the
butter and sugar. Beat the egg yolks and add with the fruit mixture to
the fat and sugar, mixing well. Mix together the flour, baking powder
and spice and add to the mixture. Stir thoroughly. Beat the egg whites
until stiff and stir in. Turn into the prepared tin and bake for 2–2½
hours until a skewer comes out clean. Remove from the oven and
leave in the tin for 30 minutes before turning out on to a wire rack
to cool.

FOR THE DECORATION

225g (8oz) apricot jam
2–3 tablespoons water
550g (1¼lb) marzipan

FOR THE ICING

3 egg whites
675g (1½lb) icing sugar, sifted
1 tablespoon lemon juice
1 teaspoon glycerine

To decorate, heat the apricot jam and water in a small pan until the jam is dissolved. Push through a sieve and place in a clean pan. Bring back to the boil and simmer until fairly thick and smooth. Brush the mixture on to the outside of the cake. On a sugared surface, roll out two-thirds of the marzipan to form a rectangle as wide as the depth of the cake and long enough to wrap all the way around it. Place around the sides of the cake and press the ends well together. Roll out the remaining marzipan to make a piece to fit the top of the cake and put in place. Press the edges well together, ensuring that the joins are neat. Leave in a warm room for 5–6 days, until the marzipan has dried.

To make the icing, beat the egg whites until very frothy. Add half the icing sugar and beat in with a wooden spoon. Add the lemon juice, the glycerine and the remaining sugar and beat until the icing forms soft peaks. Cover with a damp cloth and leave in the bowl for a few hours to allow some of the air to escape. If the icing needs thickening, add a little more sugar as necessary. Spread the icing over the cake, either smoothing it flat or brushing into soft peaks. Decorate with Christmas cake decorations, if desired.

PARADISE SLICE

The semolina in this mixture adds to the interesting variety of textures and flavours. Semolina is made by milling wheat or maize. It is unusual to include it in this type of cake. The coarse grains are more normally boiled in milk with sugar to make a sort of sweet porridge, and finely ground versions are used to make pasta and noodles.

175g (6oz) shortcrust pastry
   (see page 91)
100g (4oz) butter, softened
100g (4oz) caster sugar
1 egg, beaten
50g (2oz) semolina
50g (2oz) shredded coconut
50g (2oz) glacé cherries,
   chopped
50g (2oz) walnuts, chopped
175g (6oz) sultanas

Makes 10 slices

Make the pastry following the instructions on page 91 and chill for at least 15 minutes. Preheat the oven to 190°C, 375°F, gas mark 5. Grease an 18 x 28cm (7 x 11in) Swiss roll tin. On a lightly floured board, roll out the pastry and use to line the prepared tin. Beat together the butter and sugar until light and fluffy. Add the egg and beat again. Add the remaining ingredients and mix thoroughly. Turn into the pastry case and smooth. Bake for 20–25 minutes until golden and firm. Remove from the oven and leave to cool in the tin. When cold, cut into pieces and lift carefully from the tin.

CARROT CAKE WITH LIME TOPPING

This is another indulgent cake, which should be eaten with a pastry fork. These small, three-pronged tea forks developed from Victorian dessert forks in the second half of the 19th century. So that a little pressure could safely be exerted on a fruit tartlet or slice of Madeira cake, the first two narrow prongs of the fork were fused to make one wider prong that acted as a cutting edge. Like tea knives and silver teaspoons, the forks usually came in little boxes of six.

FOR THE CAKE

2 eggs
100g (4oz) light soft brown
    sugar
75ml (3fl oz) oil (sunflower,
    vegetable or corn)
100g (4oz) self-raising flour,
    sifted
175g (6oz) grated carrot
1 teaspoon ground cinnamon
50g (2oz) shredded coconut

FOR THE TOPPING

75g (3oz) cream cheese
75g (3oz) butter
50g (2oz) icing sugar
Grated rind of 1 lime
Toasted coconut and grated lime
    to decorate (optional)

Makes 1 x 900g (2lb) loaf or
1 x 18cm (7in) round cake

Preheat the oven to 190°C, 375°F, gas mark 5. Grease and line a 900g (2lb) loaf tin or an 18cm (7in) round tin. Beat together the eggs and sugar until very creamy. Add the oil and beat hard. Fold in the remaining ingredients and turn into the prepared tin. Smooth the top, then slightly hollow out the middle. Bake for 35–40 minutes until golden and well risen and a skewer comes out clean. Remove from the oven and turn out on to a wire rack to cool. To make the topping, beat the ingredients together until light and creamy and spread over the top of the cake. Make a pattern with the prongs of a fork. Add toasted coconut and grated lime to add colour and texture to the top, if desired.

KEDLESTON MARMALADE CAKE

Marmalades started life as a sort of quince (marmelo) jam but, in the 17th century, were made in England with oranges instead. The bittersweet flavour adds an interesting bite to this cake, which goes very well with Ceylon or Assam tea.

175g (6oz) butter, softened

50g (2oz) light or dark soft brown sugar

4 tablespoons golden syrup

2 eggs

150g (5oz) orange marmalade

275g (10oz) self-raising wholemeal flour, sifted

2 teaspoons baking powder

½ teaspoon ground ginger

3–4 tablespoons orange juice

Makes 1 x 20cm (8in) round cake

Preheat the oven to 180°C, 350°F, gas mark 4. Grease and line a 20cm (8in) round tin. Beat together the butter and sugar until light and fluffy. Add the syrup and beat again. Whisk together the eggs and marmalade and add to the mixture with the flour, baking powder and ginger. Stir in the orange juice to give a soft dropping consistency. Turn into the prepared tin and bake for about 1 hour until a skewer comes out clean. Remove from the oven and leave to cool in the tin for 15 minutes before turning out on to a wire rack to cool completely.

Right: Kedleston Marmalade Cake.
Next page: Carrot Cake with Lime Topping.

WALSINGHAM HONEY CAKE

Little Walsingham became an important place of pilgrimage when visions of the Virgin Mary were seen there, and the area has also long been famous for its bees and honey. Honey has for centuries been used to treat wounds, and it is known today that it does indeed have an antibacterial effect and therefore helps the body to heal.

225g (8oz) butter, softened
225g (8oz) light soft brown sugar
2 eggs, beaten
450g (1lb) plain flour, sifted
1 teaspoon ground ginger
1 teaspoon bicarbonate of soda
100g (4oz) raisins
50g (2oz) mixed candied peel
50g (2oz) glacé cherries, halved
300ml (10fl oz) milk
75g (3oz) clear honey
75g (3oz) black treacle
3–4 tablespoons clear honey
40g (1½oz) light soft brown
    sugar
50g (2oz) butter
50g (2oz) flaked almonds

Makes 1 x 18cm (7in)
square cake

Left: Walsingham Honey Cake.
Previous page: Banana and Fruit Cake.

Preheat the oven to 160°C, 325°F, gas mark 3. Grease and line an 18cm (7in) square tin. Beat together the butter and sugar until light and fluffy. Add the beaten eggs and beat again. Add the flour, ginger and bicarbonate of soda and beat well. Stir in the raisins, peel and cherries. Warm together the milk, honey and treacle and add gradually, beating well and making sure that all the ingredients are evenly distributed. Turn into the prepared tin and bake for 2 hours until a skewer comes out clean. Remove from the oven and leave in the tin. Warm together the honey, sugar and butter and pour over the warm cake. Sprinkle with the almonds and allow to cool completely in the tin.

BANANA AND FRUIT CAKE

This Irish recipe from Rowallane in County Down is excellent with a cup of Earl Grey. The recipe for blending bergamot with black China tea to make this very popular flavoured tea is said to have been given to a British diplomat in gratitude when he saved a mandarin's life while on a visit to China. It is said that when the diplomat returned to England, he presented it to the then Prime Minister, Earl Grey, who had the tea blended by his tea merchant and drank it as his favourite blend.

75g (3oz) butter, softened
100g (4oz) light or dark soft
   brown sugar
3 tablespoons clear honey
2 eggs, beaten
2 ripe bananas, mashed
225g (8oz) self-raising flour
1 teaspoon allspice
¼ teaspoon bicarbonate of soda
¼ teaspoon salt
225g (8oz) raisins

Makes 1 x 900g (2lb) loaf

Preheat the oven to 180°C, 350°F, gas mark 4. Grease and line a 900g (2lb) loaf tin. Beat together the butter and sugar until light and fluffy. Add the honey, eggs and bananas and beat well. Mix together the flour, allspice, bicarbonate of soda, salt and raisins and fold into the banana mixture. Mix well and then turn into the prepared tin. Bake for 1–1¼ hours until a skewer comes out clean. Remove from the oven and turn out on to a wire rack to cool.

CORNISH BANANA CAKE

When afternoon tea is set out at home the various platters of sandwiches, scones and cakes are usually arranged on a table, trolley or sideboard. In tearooms and lounges, space-saving, three-tier silver cake stands display the food and look spectacular with their neat finger sandwiches, warm scones and tiny French pastries. Dishes of jam and clotted cream are usually presented separately.

FOR THE CAKE

225g (8oz) very ripe bananas
   (weighed after peeling)
90g (3½oz) caster sugar
90g (3½oz) butter, softened
200g (7oz) self-raising flour, sifted
1 egg, beaten
½ teaspoon bicarbonate of soda
1 tablespoon milk
Whole, blanched almonds or
   dried banana chips

FOR THE FILLING

1 ripe banana
50g (2oz) butter, softened
50g (2oz) caster sugar

FOR THE ICING

1 soft, very ripe banana
25g (1oz) cocoa powder, sifted
225g (8oz) icing sugar, sifted

Makes 1 x double layer
18cm (7in) round cake

Preheat the oven to 180°C, 350°F, gas mark 4. Grease two 18cm (7in) round sandwich tins. Mash the bananas and sugar together in a food processor or mixer. Beat in the butter, and add the flour and egg alternately. Dissolve the bicarbonate of soda in the milk and add to the mixture. Beat well to a fairly sticky batter. Stir in the blanched almonds or banana chips. Turn into the prepared tins, smooth the tops and bake for 35–40 minutes, until the sponge springs back when lightly pressed. Remove from the oven and turn on to a wire rack to cool. To make the filling, beat all the ingredients together until well mixed and use to sandwich the cakes together. For the icing, beat the ingredients together until dark and really smooth and spread on to the top of the cake. Decorate with the blanched almonds, walnut halves or dried banana chips.

BANANA AND PINEAPPLE CAKE

As the ritual of teatime developed through the second half of the 19th century, households acquired more and more porcelain teaware. In the early days of tea drinking in England, little tea bowls, saucers and dishes for sugar or bread and butter were not available as matching sets, but as afternoon tea became more and more popular the idea of the tea set gradually evolved and often included 12 tea cups or bowls, 12 coffee cups, 12 saucers, side plates, larger plates for bread and butter or cakes, teapots, milk jugs and sugar basins.

5 or 6 tinned pineapple rings
200g (7oz) plain flour, sifted
1 teaspoon ground cinnamon
½ teaspoon bicarbonate of soda
200g (7oz) caster sugar
100g (4oz) pecans or walnuts,
   roughly chopped
2 bananas, mashed
1 x 432g (15¼oz) can of
   crushed pineapple, drained
100ml (4fl oz) corn or
   sunflower oil
2 eggs

Makes 1 x 23cm (9in)
ring cake

Preheat the oven to 180°C, 350°F, gas mark 4. Grease and line a 23cm (9in) ring tin and place the pineapple rings in the base of the tin. Mix together all the other ingredients and spoon into the tin. Bake for 30–35 minutes until a skewer comes out clean. Remove from the oven and leave to cool in the tin. When cold, turn out and peel off the greaseproof paper. Serve with the pineapple rings facing upwards.

PINEAPPLE UPSIDE-DOWN CAKE

A modern recipe served in the tearoom at Montacute House, an early 17th-century home whose 1728 inventory recorded two tea tables in the library. Tea tables started to appear in England in the 1680s and 90s, mostly purchased from Indonesia and Japan. In fact, so many foreign tea tables were imported that London cabinet-makers feared for their jobs and signed a petition against the practice.

175g (6oz) golden syrup
225g (8oz) tinned pineapple
  slices, drained
100g (4oz) butter, softened
100g (4oz) caster sugar
2 eggs, beaten
100g (4oz) self-raising flour,
  sifted
Pinch of salt
Pinch of ground cinnamon

Makes 1 x 15cm (6in)
round cake

Preheat the oven to 160°C, 325°F, gas mark 3. Grease and line a 15cm (6in) round tin. Spread the syrup in the base of the tin and arrange the pineapple slices over the top. Beat together the butter and sugar until light and fluffy. Beat in the eggs, one at a time, adding 1 tablespoon of flour with each. Beat hard, then fold in the remaining flour with the salt and cinnamon. Mix well without beating. Turn into the prepared tin and bake for 1¼ hours until a skewer comes out clean. Remove from the oven and leave to cool in the tin. When cold, turn out and serve with the pineapple side uppermost.

CARROT AND PINEAPPLE CAKE

English recipes have included carrots in sweet dishes and cakes since medieval times, but carrot cakes became particularly popular at teatime in the late 1960s. This one is made to a recipe from East Riddlesden Hall in West Yorkshire, where the drawing room has on show an unusual teapot in the form of a Chinese peach-shaped wine ewer. It has no lid but fills from the bottom through a long internal tube that runs upwards into the pot and stops the tea from flowing out again.

225g (8oz) rice flour
200g (7oz) caster sugar
½ teaspoon salt
½ teaspoon bicarbonate of soda
100g (4oz) undrained crushed
     pineapple
200g (7oz) grated carrot
100ml (4fl oz) corn or
     vegetable oil
2 eggs, beaten
½ teaspoon vanilla essence
50g (2oz) walnuts, roughly
     chopped

Makes 1 x 900g (2lb) loaf

Preheat the oven to 190°C, 375°F, gas mark 5. Grease and line a 900g (2lb) loaf tin. Mix together the flour, sugar, salt and bicarbonate of soda. Add the pineapple, carrot, oil, eggs, vanilla essence and walnuts and mix thoroughly. Turn into the prepared tin and bake for 1–1½ hours until a skewer comes out clean. Remove from the oven and leave to cool in the tin for a few minutes before turning out on to a wire rack to cool completely.

AMERICAN ZUCCHINI CAKE

Zucchini, or courgettes, are an unusual ingredient in a cake but, like carrots, they make the dough soft and moist. This recipe is from Hidcote Manor Garden in Gloucestershire where it is said the National Trust first served teas to members of the public. The tea was brewed in the gardener's cottage and handed out through the window to thirsty visitors.

2 eggs
100ml (4fl oz) oil (corn,
    vegetable or sunflower)
225g (8oz) caster sugar
350g (12oz) grated courgettes
1½ teaspoons vanilla or almond
    essence
50g (2oz) chopped nuts or a
    mixture of 25g (1oz)
    chopped nuts and 25g (1oz)
    sultanas
175g (6oz) self-raising flour,
    sifted
1½ teaspoons ground cinnamon
    or mixed spice

Makes 1 x 900g (2lb) loaf

Preheat the oven to 160°C, 325°F, gas mark 3. Grease and line a 900g (2lb) loaf tin. Beat the eggs until light and foamy. Add the oil, sugar, courgettes and essence and mix lightly, until all the ingredients are evenly distributed. Fold in the nuts (or nuts and sultanas), flour and spice until well mixed and turn into the prepared tin. Bake for 1¼–1½ hours until a skewer comes out clean. Remove from the oven and turn out on to a wire rack to cool.

STICKY LEMON CAKE

This wonderfully tangy cake is made to a recipe from Castle Drogo in Devon which was built by Julius Drewe in 1900 to Sir Edwin Lutyens' design. Mr Drewe opened his own tea store (the Willow Pattern Tea Store) in 1878, then set up the Home and Colonial Stores in 1883, and sold so much tea that he became a millionaire. While he lived at Castle Drogo, tea was served each day in the library and was 'a wonderful meal with wafer-thin bread and butter, scones and jam and Devonshire cream'.

FOR THE CAKE
100g (4oz) butter, softened
100g (4oz) caster sugar
2 eggs
100g (4oz) self-raising flour,
    sifted
Grated rind and juice of
    half a lemon
1½ tablespoons icing sugar, sifted

FOR THE ICING
50–75g (2–3oz) icing sugar, sifted
Juice and finely grated rind of
    half a lemon

Makes 1 x 18cm (7in)
round cake

Preheat the oven to 160°C, 325°F, gas mark 3. Grease and line an 18cm (7in) round tin. Beat together the butter and sugar until light and fluffy. Beat in the eggs, one at a time, whisking hard after the addition of each one. Fold in the flour and rind, mix well and turn into the prepared tin. Bake for 45 minutes until a skewer comes out clean. Remove from the oven and make several holes in the top of the cake with a skewer. Mix together the icing sugar and lemon juice and pour over the cake. Leave in the tin until absolutely cold. Meanwhile make the icing. Mix together the icing sugar and the lemon rind and juice. When the cake is cold, turn out and ice with the prepared mixture.

ORANGE AND LEMON CAKE

Invitations to afternoon tea were issued verbally or by a small card delivered one or two days before. No answer was required. On the subject of the correct time to arrive, one writer of etiquette books advised that 'the proper time is from four to seven'. Guests were not expected to stay throughout but to come and go as they pleased.

225g (8oz) butter, softened
225g (8oz) caster sugar
3 eggs
Juice and rind of half an orange
Juice and rind of half a lemon
225g (8oz) plain flour, sifted

Makes 1 x 20cm (8in)
round cake

Preheat the oven to 160°C, 325°F, gas mark 3. Grease and line a 20cm (8in) round tin. Beat together the butter and sugar until light and fluffy. Add the eggs, orange and lemon rind and juice and beat well. Add the flour and beat carefully for a few seconds. Turn into the prepared tin and bake for 1 hour until a skewer comes out clean. Remove from the oven and leave to cool in the tin.

    If desired, split in half and fill with butter filling made with the grated rind and juice from half a lemon and half an orange, 50g (2oz) softened butter and 175g (6oz) sifted icing sugar. Decorate the top by dusting with icing sugar or spread with glacé icing made by mixing together 175g (6oz) icing sugar and the juice and grated rind of half a lemon and half an orange.

SUSSEX APPLE CAKE

Sticky fingers from eating cakes like this demand elegant linen tea napkins. As early as 1773, inventories of household linens included such entries as '4 dozen Bird Eye Tea Napkens' (napkins made in two-colour, double-knit fabric). Victorian tea linens were often in white lace or linen decorated with drawn-thread work or embroidery, while the Edwardians seem to have preferred a cream-coloured background for their pretty tea sets.

225g (8oz) butter, softened

225g (8oz) dark soft brown sugar

3 large eggs

150g (5oz) walnuts, finely chopped or crushed

150g (5oz) sultanas or raisins

225g (8oz) wholemeal self-raising flour, sifted

400g (14oz) cooking apples, peeled, cored and grated

½ teaspoon ground cloves

Makes 1 x 23cm (9in) round cake

Preheat the oven to 180°C, 350°F, gas mark 4. Grease and line the base of a 23cm (9in) loose-bottomed round tin. Beat together the butter and 175g (6oz) of the sugar until light and fluffy. Add the eggs and beat hard. Fold in 100g (4oz) of the walnuts, the sultanas or raisins and the flour, mixing well so that all the ingredients are evenly distributed. Put half the mixture into the prepared tin. Mix together the apples and cloves and spread over the layer of cake mixture. Spread the remaining cake mixture on top and smooth with a palette knife. Mix together the remaining sugar and walnuts and sprinkle evenly over the top of the cake. Bake for 1¼–1½ hours until the top is caramelised but not too brown. Remove from the oven and leave to cool in the tin.

PRATIE CAKE

Like so many Irish recipes, this cake relies on potatoes but adds apples, brown sugar and butter to create a juicy, fruity, double-layer, pie-like treat. It is best served hot straight from the oven with a strong cup of Irish breakfast blend or a strong Assam or Ceylon tea.

450g (1lb) potatoes, boiled and
  mashed
1 teaspoon salt
50g (2oz) butter, melted
4 tablespoons plain flour, sifted
4–6 cooking apples, peeled,
  cored and sliced
2 tablespoons demerara or light
  soft brown sugar
A little milk
25–50g (1–2oz) butter
Demerara or caster sugar for
  dredging

Makes 1 x 18cm (7in)
round cake

Preheat the oven to 190°C, 375°F, gas mark 5. Grease a baking tray. Mix together the mashed potatoes, salt and butter and work in the flour to give a pliable dough. Knead lightly, then divide into two portions. On a floured board, roll each piece out into a round approximately 18cm (7in) in diameter, making one slightly larger than the other. Place the larger round on the baking tray and lay the apple slices on top of the dough. Sprinkle with the sugar. Dampen the edges of the dough with a little milk and lay the other round on top. Press the edges well together. Bake for 45–60 minutes until the apples are tender and the top is golden. Remove from the oven, spread with butter, dredge all over with sugar and serve hot.

If liked, add half a teaspoon of ground ginger to the mixture with the flour, and, if you prefer a slightly sweeter cake, also add a little caster sugar.

APPLECAKE FINGERS

This is an easy recipe from Anglesey Abbey in Cambridgeshire. In the house, there is an interesting piece of Ming porcelain that started life as a ginger jar and was later converted into a teapot. It stands about 18cm (7in) tall and is made of brown clay slipware decorated with a cream-coloured design on each side. A delicate silver spout and handle have been added, a silver cherub stands on top of the lid and the jar sits on a fine silver mount. The pot is Chinese and the silver additions would have been fashioned and fitted in Europe.

FOR THE CAKE
150g (5oz) plain flour, sifted
150g (5oz) sugar
½ teaspoon baking powder
½ teaspoon mixed spice
Pinch of salt
90g (3½oz) butter, softened
1 large egg, beaten
75ml (3fl oz) milk
65g (2½oz) cooking or eating
    apples, chopped

FOR THE GLAZE
175–225g (6–8oz) icing sugar,
    sifted
1½–2 tablespoons water
A few drops of lemon juice and
    a little grated lemon rind
    (optional)

Makes 15 pieces

Preheat the oven to 190°C, 375°F, gas mark 5. Grease a 18 x 28cm (7 x 11in) Swiss roll tin. Mix together the flour, sugar, baking powder, spice and salt and rub in the butter until the mixture resembles fine breadcrumbs. Add the beaten egg and milk and mix until smooth. Add the chopped apple and mix so that it is evenly distributed. Press into the prepared tin and bake for approximately 35 minutes until golden and firm. Remove from the oven and leave to cool in the tin. When cold, mix together the icing sugar, water, lemon juice and rind, if using, and pour the icing over the top of the cake. Leave to set, then cut the cake into fingers and lift carefully from the tin.

SUFFOLK APPLE CAKE

This is a traditional cake from a county that has always been an important apple-growing area of England. And when it's time to brew a pot of tea to go with it, remember that there are thousands of different teas made around the world in more than 35 countries and every single one of them is different. Just as different grape varietals give different wine characters, so the different cultivars of the tea bush have their own individual flavour and aroma. And with the huge variety, there is a tea to suit all palates.

225g (8oz) plain flour, sifted
1½ teaspoons baking powder
Pinch of salt
100g (4oz) lard or dripping
225g (8oz) eating apples
    (weighed after being
    peeled and cored), finely
    chopped or grated
1½ tablespoons caster,
    granulated or demerara sugar
1–2 tablespoons milk

Makes 1 x 20cm (8in)
round cake

Preheat the oven to 180°C, 350°F, gas mark 4. Grease a baking tray. Mix together the flour, baking powder and salt and rub in the fat. Add the apples, sugar and enough milk to give a soft dough. Place the dough on the prepared tray and shape by hand into a flat round cake approximately 20cm (8in) across and 1–1.5cm (½–¾in) thick. Bake for 40–45 minutes until golden and firm. Remove from the oven and serve hot, split and buttered.

CHESHIRE SOULING CAKES

Souling cakes were baked for All Souls' Day when children went around the villages begging for sustenance.
The cakes are thought to have descended from the food that was left out in graves for the dead in pagan days.

350g (12oz) plain flour, sifted
½ teaspoon ground cinnamon
½ teaspoon mixed spice
Pinch of nutmeg
175g (6oz) caster sugar
175g (6oz) butter, softened
1 egg, beaten
1½ teaspoons white
   wine vinegar

Makes approximately 26 cakes

Preheat the oven to 180°C, 350°F, gas mark 4. Grease two baking trays. Mix together all the dry ingredients and rub in the butter. Add the beaten egg and vinegar and mix to a soft dough. Knead gently until smooth. On a lightly floured board, roll out to a thickness of 0.5cm (¼in) and cut into rounds with a 7.5cm (3in) cutter. Place on the prepared trays and bake for 15–20 minutes until lightly browned. Remove from the oven and leave to cool on the trays for a few minutes, before lifting carefully on to a wire rack to cool completely.

STREUSEL CRUNCHY CAKE

Using muesli as one of the ingredients, this spiced, nutty cake has a wonderful texture and layers of interesting flavours. Muesli is generally considered to be a healthy food because it contains oats, which help to reduce blood cholesterol, and nuts, which are rich in omega-3 fatty acids and are good for the nervous system.

FOR THE CAKE
150g (5oz) self-raising flour,
    sifted
150g (5oz) light soft brown
    sugar
175g (6oz) butter, softened
3 eggs, beaten

FOR THE FILLING AND
    TOPPING
2 tablespoons muesli cereal
1 tablespoon light soft brown
    sugar
1 teaspoon ground cinnamon
50g (2oz) walnuts, roughly
    chopped

Makes 1 x 18cm (7in)
round cake

Preheat the oven to 180°C, 350°F, gas mark 4. Grease and line a 18cm (7in) loose-bottomed round tin. Place the flour, sugar, butter and eggs together in a bowl and beat for 2 minutes. Turn half the mixture into the prepared tin and press down. Mix together the ingredients for the filling and topping and sprinkle two-thirds over the cake. Spread the remaining cake mixture on top and smooth. Sprinkle the remaining muesli mixture over the top and bake for 20–25 minutes until firm and browned. Remove from the oven and leave to cool in the tin.

DANIEL'S COFFEE AND DRAMBUIE MERINGUES

This luxurious recipe comes from Fountains Abbey and Studley Royal, which boasts a beautiful naturalistic park that surrounds the Abbey. The Banqueting House was originally intended for the consumption of sweetmeats, fruit and sweet wines after dinner, but during the 18th century buildings like this were more frequently used as a venue for a tea party.

4 egg whites
225g (8oz) caster sugar
1 teaspoon cornflour
1 teaspoon vanilla essence
½ teaspoon white wine vinegar
300ml (10fl oz) double cream,
   whipped
3 tablespoons Drambuie
1 teaspoon finely ground coffee
8 walnut halves

Makes 8 meringue nests

Preheat the oven to 110°C, 225°F, gas mark ¼. Cover a baking tray with greaseproof paper. Whisk the egg whites with 100g (4oz) of the sugar until very stiff. Add another 100g (4oz) of sugar and whisk again. Add the cornflour, vanilla essence and vinegar and fold carefully in. Place the mixture in a large piping bag fitted with a 1cm (½in) star nozzle and pipe eight nests on to the greaseproof paper. Bake for 1 hour, then reduce the oven temperature to the lowest possible setting and bake for 4 hours more. Remove from the oven and leave to cool. If not needed immediately, place in an airtight container. When ready to use, mix together the whipped cream, Drambuie and coffee and place in a piping bag. Pipe the cream into the nests and decorate each with a half walnut.

Right: Daniel's Coffee and Drambuie Meringues.

APRICOT SWISS ROLL

Apricots and almonds go exceptionally well together in this luxurious, creamy rolled sponge, which makes a mouthwatering dessert or a very special cake for tea. To eat it without ending up with very sticky fingers, little tea knives or pastry forks are needed. In the Edwardian period, the heyday for tea, several new pieces of tea equipage were developed, including sets of pastry forks, tea knives, muffin dishes for keeping buttered muffins and crumpets hot, and muffineers, invented for shaking cinnamon sugar on to buttered toast.

FOR THE SPONGE
2 eggs
75g (3oz) caster sugar
75g (3oz) self-raising flour, sifted
Caster sugar for dusting

FOR THE FILLING
1 x 410g (14½oz) tin apricots,
    drained and the juice
    reserved
1–2 tablespoons brandy
150ml (5fl oz) whipped cream
25g (1oz) flaked almonds,
    untoasted
25g (1oz) flaked almonds,
    toasted
Icing sugar for dusting

Serves 6

To make the sponge, preheat the oven to 160°C, 325°F, gas mark 3. Grease and line a 18 x 28cm (7 x 11in) Swiss roll tin. Beat the eggs thoroughly. Add the sugar and continue beating until thick and mousse-like. Fold in the flour and turn into the prepared tin. Bake for 10–15 minutes until the sponge springs back when lightly pressed. Remove from the oven and invert the tin on to a clean teacloth dusted with a little caster sugar. Roll the sponge immediately round a wooden rolling pin or a milk bottle and leave to cool. Meanwhile slice the apricots and soak in the brandy. Just before serving, carefully unroll the sponge and spread with the whipped cream. Arrange the apricots over the top and pour on the brandy and apricot mix. Sprinkle with the untoasted almonds and carefully roll the sponge up again. Place on a serving dish, pour a little of the reserved apricot juice over the sponge, sprinkle the top with toasted almonds and dust with icing sugar. Serve immediately.

Left: Apricot Swiss Roll.

DOLCE TORINESE

This rich, flavoursome cake makes an excellent dessert for a special dinner party. The almonds give it a lovely nutty texture, and are rich in vitamins, fibre, magnesium and antioxidants. In fact they are thought to contain similar levels of antioxidants to broccoli and tea. And a slice of Dolce Torinese is much nicer with a fresh cup of tea than a plateful of broccoli! This recipe contains raw egg.

100g (4oz) good-quality plain
    chocolate
1½ tablespoons sherry, brandy
    or rum
100g (4oz) unsalted butter,
    softened
150g (5oz) caster sugar
1 egg, separated
65g (2½oz) blanched almonds,
    shredded
6 butter biscuits, broken into
    small pieces
Icing sugar for dusting
Whipped cream (optional)

Makes 1 x 20cm (8in)
round cake

Grease and line a 20cm (8in) round, loose-bottomed tin. Melt the chocolate and stir in the alcohol. Beat the butter, sugar and egg yolk until light and fluffy. Stir in the almonds and the chocolate mixture. Beat the egg white until very stiff and fold into the mixture. Add the broken biscuits and stir until evenly distributed. Turn into the prepared tin and smooth the top. Place the tin in the refrigerator and leave to set overnight. When ready to serve, turn out and dust with icing sugar. If liked, pipe some whipped cream around the edge, or serve separately.

CANONS ASHBY COCONUT CAKE

Canons Ashby in Northamptonshire was once famous for its local postman, who doubled as hedge-clipper. One day when the owner, Sir Henry Dryden, was having a tea party on the lawn with his friends, he asked the postman to clip the yew trees while he was on the premises. As the guests watched him clip away, they decided to ask him to exercise his skills and give them each a haircut and, having performed the task to their satisfaction, he then joined the tea party!

FOR THE CAKE
100g (4oz) butter, softened
75g (3oz) light soft brown sugar
2 teaspoons almond essence
Grated rind of 1 lemon
1 egg, beaten
250g (9oz) plain flour, sifted
5–6 tablespoons plum jam

FOR THE TOPPING
1 egg, beaten
75g (3oz) light soft brown sugar
100g (4oz) shredded coconut

FOR DIPPING
175–225g (6–8oz) milk or
    plain chocolate

Makes 12 fingers

Preheat the oven to 180°C, 350°F, gas mark 4. Grease an 18 x 28cm (7 x 11in) Swiss roll tin. Beat together the butter, sugar, almond essence, lemon rind and egg. Add the flour and mix well. Press into the prepared tin and spread a layer of jam on top. Mix together the ingredients for the topping and spread over the jam. Bake for 20–30 minutes until firm and pale golden. Remove from the oven and leave to cool in the tin. When cold, cut into fingers and lift carefully from the tin. Melt the chocolate and dip both ends of each finger into it. Place carefully on a wire rack to set.

TARTS AND FLANS

The British love their pastry and over the centuries have filled short and flaky pastry cases with creamy egg custards, lemon and curd cheese mixtures, buttery and spiced dried fruit blends and whatever fresh fruits are in season. As well as featuring on the tea table, many of these recipes can double as desserts served with whipped cream or delicious, velvety custard.

WILFRA APPLE CAKE

One of Yorkshire's best-known pastries, this was baked in Ripon on St Wilfrid's Day (the first or second Saturday of August) to celebrate the return of the saint to his home town after a long absence abroad. Another favourite for the same festivity were little Wilfra Tarts, which the residents of the town would make by the dozen and place outside their front doors so that passers-by could help themselves.

450g (1lb) shortcrust pastry
(see page 91)
900g (2lb) cooking apples,
peeled, cored and sliced
75–100g (3–4oz) granulated,
demerara or soft brown
sugar
50–75g (2–3oz) Wensleydale
cheese, grated
Milk or beaten egg to glaze

Makes 1 x 18 x 28cm
(7 x 11in) tart

Make the pastry following the instructions on page 91 and chill for at least 15 minutes. Preheat the oven to 190°C, 375°F, gas mark 5. Grease a 18 x 28cm (7 x 11in) Swiss roll tin. Cook the apples gently in a pan with the sugar until just soft. On a floured board, roll out half the pastry to make a rectangle to fit the tin and use to line the base and sides. Pour in the apples and spread evenly. Sprinkle the cheese over the apples. Roll out the remaining pastry and place on top of the cheese. Brush the edges with a little milk and seal well. Brush the top with milk or beaten egg and bake for 30–35 minutes until golden. Remove from the oven and allow to cool in the tin. When cold, cut into slabs and lift carefully from the tin.

SPICY APPLE FLAN

Suffolk was once an important apple-growing region, with orchards mainly found in the east and south of the county. Most of the apple producers owned smallholdings and sent their crop to the London markets by rail or road. The most famous of the local apples is the St Edmund's Russet, named for Saint Edmund, Saxon king of the East Angles in the 9th century AD.

FOR THE BASE
175g (6oz) self-raising flour, sifted
100g (4oz) butter, softened
1 egg, beaten
40g (1½oz) granulated or light or dark soft brown sugar
Pinch of salt

FOR THE TOPPING
5 large cooking apples, peeled, cored and sliced
50g (2oz) sugar
1 teaspoon mixed spice
50g (2oz) sultanas

Makes 8 portions

Preheat the oven to 180°C, 350°F, gas mark 4. Grease an 18cm (7in) round tin. Using a fork or electric beater, mix together the ingredients for the base and, on a lightly floured board, roll out to make a circle to fit the tin. Place in the tin and press well against the edges. Arrange the apples in layers on top of the dough, sprinkling some of the sugar, spice and sultanas on each layer. Bake for 1 hour, watching carefully, until the top is browned and the apples are tender. Remove from the oven and leave to cool in the tin.

LANCASTER LEMON TART

In the early days of tea drinking in England, tea was served as an after-dinner 'digestif'. When the last morsels of food had been consumed, the company would retire to a drawing room, where the tea table had been prepared by the servants. The lady of the house would set the silver kettle to boil, take her tea jar from the shelf, warm the teapot, then measure in the tea and pour on the boiling water. She would then pour the brew into handleless porcelain bowls and hand them around to her family and friends.

175g (6oz) shortcrust pastry
  (see page 91)
150–175g (5–6oz) lemon curd
100g (4oz) butter, softened
100g (4oz) caster sugar
2 eggs, beaten
3 teaspoons lemon juice
75g (3oz) self-raising flour, sifted
25g (1oz) ground almonds

Makes 1 x 20cm (8in) round tart

Make the pastry following the instructions on page 91 and chill for at least 15 minutes. Preheat the oven to 180°C, 350°F, gas mark 4. Grease a 20cm (8in) loose-bottomed round flan tin. On a floured board, roll out the pastry and use to line the tin. Spread the lemon curd over the base. Beat together the butter and sugar until pale and fluffy. Gradually add the beaten eggs and the lemon juice and beat well. Add the flour and ground almonds and fold in with a metal spoon. Spread the mixture over the lemon curd and smooth out. Bake for 35 minutes, then reduce the oven temperature to 150°C, 300°F, gas mark 2 and bake for 10–15 minutes more until the sponge springs back when lightly pressed. Remove from the oven and leave to cool in the tin. When cold, cut into pieces.

Right: Lancaster Lemon Tart.
Next page: Spicy Apple Flan.

MANCHESTER TART

This meringue-topped tart is a little like a Queen of Puddings in a pastry shell. The recipe comes from Dunham Massey in Cheshire, where the 'tea room' in the house holds rare tea and coffee tables, the family silver teawares and two tall tea caddies of japanned metal inlaid with mother of pearl. These large tins would have held the main supply of loose-leaf tea and smaller caddies, now on show on side tables and mantel shelves in the drawing and dining rooms, would have been regularly replenished.

175g (6oz) flaky pastry
   (see page 89)
3–4 tablespoons raspberry or
   strawberry jam
Rind of 1 lemon, cut into strips
300ml (10fl oz) milk
50g (2oz) fresh breadcrumbs
50g (2oz) butter, softened
2 eggs, separated
75g (3oz) caster sugar
1 tablespoon brandy
Caster sugar for dusting

Makes 1 x 20cm (8in)
round tart

Make the pastry following the instructions on page 89 and chill for at least 45 minutes. Preheat the oven to 190°C, 375°F, gas mark 5. Grease and line an 20cm (8in) round pie dish or loose-bottomed round tin. On a floured board, roll out the pastry and use to line the prepared tin. Spread the jam over the base. Put the lemon rind and milk into a pan and bring to the boil. Remove from the heat and strain on to the breadcrumbs. Leave to stand for 5 minutes. Add the butter, egg yolks, 25g (1oz) of the sugar and the brandy and beat well. Pour into the pastry case and bake for 45 minutes. Meanwhile whisk the egg whites until stiff and fold in the remaining 50g (2oz) of sugar. Remove the tart from the oven and spread the meringue over the filling. Dust with caster sugar and bake for a further 15 minutes, until the meringue is brown. Remove from the oven and leave to cool. Serve cold with cream.

Left: Manchester Tart.
Previous page: Cherry Bakewells.

CHERRY BAKEWELLS

Bakewell tarts descend from what were originally called Bakewell puddings, said to date back to the 16th century and to have been invented by accident when a cook at a local inn misunderstood her employee's instructions to make a strawberry tart. Apparently, instead of adding eggs and sugar to the pastry, she beat them up with a secret ingredient and spread the mixture over the strawberries. Today, the recipe calls for strawberry jam instead of fresh fruit and sometimes decorates the top with a little icing and a cherry.

225g (8oz) shortcrust pastry
   (see page 91)
50g (2oz) strawberry jam
100g (4oz) butter, softened
100g (4oz) caster sugar
2 eggs
50g (2oz) ground almonds
50g (2oz) self-raising four, sifted
1 teaspoon almond essence
175g (6oz) icing sugar, sifted
1–2 tablespoons water
20 cherries (fresh, stoned
   or glacé)

Makes 20 tarts

Make the pastry following the instructions on page 91 and chill for at least 15 minutes. Preheat the oven to 200°C, 400°F, gas mark 6. Grease 20 patty tins. On a lightly floured board, roll out the pastry and cut twenty circles using a 7.5cm (3in) cutter. Use to line the prepared tins and spread a little jam in the base of each. Beat together the butter and caster sugar, then beat in the eggs, one at a time, adding half the ground almonds after each one. Add the flour and almond essence and stir well. Spoon the mixture into the pastry cases and bake for 20 minutes until well risen, firm and golden. Remove from the oven and leave to cool in the tins. Mix together the icing sugar and water and, when the tarts are cold, spoon the icing on to the top. Decorate each with a cherry.

SECRETARY TARTS

These oddly named tartlets are served in the tearoom at Polesden Lacey in Surrey, a Regency house with strong links to afternoon tea rituals. Hosted by Mrs Ronnie Greville, the elegant and renowned society hostess, tea was an important part of the famous parties held from 1906 until the outbreak of World War II. Guests included Indian maharajahs, literary figures such as Harold Nicolson, prominent politicians and royalty, including Edward VII and the honeymooning future George VI and Queen Elizabeth.

450g (1lb) rich shortcrust or
   shortcrust pastry (see page
   90 or 91)
175g (6oz) butter
175g (6oz) light soft brown
   sugar
1 x 405g (14oz) large can
   condensed milk
50g (2oz) walnuts, roughly
   chopped
50g (2oz) raisins

Makes 24 tarts

Make the pastry following the instructions on page 90 or 91 and chill for at least 15 minutes. Preheat the oven to 230°C, 450°F, gas mark 8. Grease 24 patty tins. On a floured board, roll out the pastry to a thickness of 0.5cm (¼in) and cut 24 circles using a 7.5cm (3in) fluted cutter. Use to line the prepared patty tins. Place little squares of greaseproof paper in each tart and fill with baking beans. Bake blind for 10 minutes. Remove from the oven, lift the baking beans and paper out of the cases and return to the oven for a further 5 minutes. Remove and turn off the oven. Put the butter, sugar and milk into a medium-sized pan and bring to the boil. Boil hard for 7 minutes, stirring all the time, until the mixture becomes a caramel colour. Remove from the heat and allow to cool for 5 minutes. Stir in the walnuts and raisins and spoon into the pastry cases. Put into the refrigerator to set.

KENTISH PUDDING PIES

These little tarts are typical of the cheesecakes and egg custards that were popular in England as far back as the 17th century. Until the 19th century, eggs, like all animal products, were forbidden during the Lenten fast. The hens, of course, went on laying during Lent, and the surplus of eggs was used over the Easter weekend in egg custards and tarts. In Kent these would be eaten with cherry beer – ale with cherry juice added.

450g (1lb) shortcrust pastry
   (see page 91)
600ml (1 pint) milk
3 strips of lemon rind
100g (4oz) butter
75g (3oz) caster sugar
2 eggs, beaten
50g (2oz) ground rice
Pinch of salt
Juice of half a lemon
50g (2oz) currants

Makes 24 tarts

Make the pastry following the instructions on page 91 and chill for 15 minutes. Put the milk and lemon rind in a pan and stand it over a gentle heat for about 20 minutes. Meanwhile preheat the oven to 180°C, 350°F, gas mark 4. Grease 24 patty tins. On a floured board, roll out the pastry to a thickness of 0.5cm (¼in) and cut 24 circles using a 7.5cm (3in) cutter. Line the prepared patty tins with the pastry circles. Remove the strips of lemon rind from the milk and discard. Add the butter and 50g (2oz) of the sugar to the milk and stir well. Mix together the beaten eggs, the ground rice, salt and lemon juice and add to the saucepan. Stir over a gentle heat until the mixture begins to thicken. Stir in the currants. Spoon the mixture into the pastry cases and sprinkle with the remaining sugar. Bake for 25–30 minutes until the pastry is golden and the filling is firm and well risen. Remove from the oven and leave to cool in the tins.

YORKSHIRE CURD TART

Open curd-cheese tarts and cheesecakes have been favourite puddings in Yorkshire for centuries, and were often served as Easter specialities to use up some of the plentiful eggs and curd cheese available after the Lenten fast.

175g (6oz) shortcrust pastry
 (see page 91)
50g (2oz) butter, softened
50g (2oz) caster sugar
1 egg, beaten
50g (2oz) currants
100g (4oz) cottage cheese
50g (2oz) sponge or biscuit
 crumbs
Grated rind and juice of
 1 lemon
½ teaspoon grated nutmeg

Makes 1 x 20cm (8in) round tart

Make the pastry following the instructions on page 91 and chill for at least 15 minutes. Preheat the oven to 190°C, 375°F, gas mark 5. Grease a 20cm (8in) round flan dish or tin. On a floured board, roll out the pastry to make a circle to fit the prepared tin or dish and use to line the base and sides. Beat together the butter and sugar until light and fluffy. Add the beaten egg and beat hard. Add the currants, cottage cheese, sponge or biscuit crumbs, lemon rind and juice and the nutmeg and beat again. Turn into the pastry case, smooth and bake for 20–25 minutes until golden. Remove from the oven and serve warm or cold with thick cream.

LONGSHAW TART

Named after the estate near Sheffield where this recipe comes from, the tart is a version of Bakewell tart, another local speciality. This may well have featured on the 'high tea' table when the family arrived home hungry at the end of the working day. Whereas 'afternoon tea' was also called 'low tea' (because one sat in low armchairs and chaise longues) or 'handed tea' (because the cups of tea were handed around by the hostess), 'high tea' was also called 'meat tea' and 'great tea'.

350g (12oz) shortcrust pastry
   (see page 91)
6–7 tablespoons jam (raspberry,
   strawberry or apricot)
250g (9oz) butter, softened
250g (9oz) granulated sugar
115g (4½oz) peanuts, finely
   chopped
115g (4½oz) fresh breadcrumbs
   (white or wholemeal)
3 eggs, beaten
1½ teaspoons almond essence

Makes 20 slices

Make the pastry following the instructions on page 91 and chill for at least 15 minutes. Preheat the oven to 190°C, 375°F, gas mark 5. Grease a 25 x 30 x 3.5cm (10 x 12 x 1½in) tin. On a floured board, roll out the pastry to make a rectangle to fit the tin and use to line the base. Spread the jam over the pastry. Beat together the butter and sugar until light and fluffy. Add the peanuts, breadcrumbs, beaten eggs and almond essence and mix well. Turn into the pastry case and bake for 25–30 minutes until firm and golden. Remove from the oven and leave to cool in the tin. When cold, cut into slices and lift carefully out of the tin.

LAKELAND COCONUT TART

Instead of the almonds used in the frangipani topping for Bakewell tart and the peanuts in Longshaw tart (see opposite), this pastry-based teatime treat includes coconut. The recipe comes from Quarry Bank Mill in Cheshire which thrived as a result of the burgeoning cotton industry of the 18th century and provided schools and apprenticeship houses for the children who made up a third of the workforce. The staple diet of an average worker was potatoes and wheaten bread, washed down with tea or coffee.

175g (6oz) shortcrust pastry
   (see page 91)
3–4 tablespoons strawberry
   or raspberry jam
100g (4oz) butter
50g (2oz) caster sugar
2 level tablespoons golden syrup
225g (8oz) shredded coconut
2 eggs, beaten

Makes 1 x 20cm (8in) round tart

Make the pastry following the instructions on page 91 and chill for at least 15 minutes. Preheat the oven to 190°C, 375°F, gas mark 5. Grease a 20cm (8in) round flan tin or a deep pie plate. On a floured board, roll out the pastry and use to line the prepared tin. Spread the jam over the pastry base. Melt together the butter, sugar and syrup and stir in the coconut and beaten eggs. Turn into the pastry case and bake in the middle of the oven for 30 minutes until golden (this tart browns and burns easily, so cover with foil after the first 10 minutes of baking time). Remove from the oven and leave to cool in the tin.

TREACLE TART

Beningbrough Hall near York serves this sticky, indulgent tart in its tearoom. The house has a closet on the ground floor as part of a grand suite of rooms used by honoured guests. Always richly decorated, the closet was often used to entertain visitors to tea, and all the porcelain teapots, bowls and dishes required to brew and serve tea were displayed on shelves and ledges over the fireplace. The tea was too expensive to leave in charge of the servants so it was also kept here, in little porcelain jars imported from China.

FOR THE PASTRY
50g (2oz) lard or other
    shortening, softened
50g (2oz) butter, softened
225g (8oz) plain flour, sifted
25g (1oz) caster sugar
A little cold water

FOR THE FILLING
450g (1lb) golden syrup
100–175g (4–6oz) fresh white
    breadcrumbs
Juice of half a lemon

Makes 12 portions

Make the pastry by rubbing the fats into the flour. Add the sugar and enough water to mix to a soft but pliable dough. Knead lightly, wrap in foil or clingfilm and chill for at least 15 minutes. Preheat the oven to 180°C, 350°F, gas mark 4. Grease a 30cm (12in) round flan dish. On a floured board, roll out the pastry to fit the prepared dish and use to line the base and sides. Place the syrup in a pan and warm gently. Remove from the heat, add the breadcrumbs and lemon juice and leave until the bread is well soaked. If the mixture is dry, add a little more syrup. Turn the mixture into the pastry case and spread evenly. Bake for 25–30 minutes until the pastry is golden and the filling nicely browned. Remove from the oven and serve warm or cold with cream or ice cream, if desired.

MAIDS OF HONOUR

Surrey's Maids of Honour started life at Hampton Court in the days of Henry VIII. According to legend, one day the king came across some of Anne Boleyn's maids enjoying some little tartlets and asked if he could try one. He declared it so good that the recipe must be kept only for royal consumption. Then in the reign of George I, it is said that a lady at court gave the secret recipe to a gentleman who set up shop in Richmond where he baked and sold the tarts. In 1951, the recipe was made public.

450g (1lb) rich shortcrust pastry
(see page 90)
100g (4oz) curd cheese
75g (3oz) butter, softened
2 eggs, beaten
65ml (2½fl oz) brandy
75g (3oz) caster sugar
75g (3oz) cold mashed potatoes
25g (1oz) ground almonds
½ teaspoon grated nutmeg
Grated rind of 2 lemons
Juice of 1 lemon

Makes approximately 24 tarts

Make the pastry following the instructions on page 90 and chill for at least 15 minutes. Preheat the oven to 180°C, 350°F, gas mark 4. Grease 24 patty tins. On a lightly floured board, roll out the pastry and cut 24 circles using a 7.5cm (3in) cutter. Use to line the prepared patty tins. Beat together the curd cheese and butter. Add the beaten eggs, brandy and sugar and beat again. In a separate bowl beat together the mashed potatoes, ground almonds, nutmeg, lemon rind and juice, and gradually mix in the cheese mixture. Beat thoroughly. Spoon into the pastry cases and bake for 35–40 minutes until risen, golden and firm. Remove from the oven and leave to cool in the tins for 5–10 minutes before lifting carefully on to a wire rack to finish cooling completely.

SLY CAKE

Several of Yorkshire's local specialities have acquired odd names over the centuries. Yorkshire Moggie is a kind of gingerbread, Stottie Cake is a flat bread, and Sly Cake fills a flat pastry case with dried fruits, walnuts, sugar and butter. Although foreign visitors may attempt to eat such sticky sweetmeats with knife and fork at teatime, British etiquette demands that we use either a pastry fork, held in the right hand, or our fingers, perhaps assisted by a small tea knife. We never use both together at teatime.

350–400g (12–14oz) shortcrust pastry (see page 91)

175g (6oz) stoned dates, chopped

50g (2oz) raisins

50g (2oz) currants

50g (2oz) walnuts, chopped

50g (2oz) light or dark soft brown sugar

4 tablespoons water

50g (2oz) butter

1–2 tablespoons milk

2 tablespoons demerara sugar, for dusting

Makes 8–10 pieces

Make the pastry following the instructions on page 91 and chill for at least 15 minutes. Preheat the oven to 190°C, 375°F, gas mark 5. Grease a tin measuring approximately 10 x 23cm (4 x 9in). On a floured board, roll out half the pastry and use to line the base and sides of the tin. Put the dates, raisins, currants, walnuts, sugar, water and butter into a pan, bring to the boil and simmer for 10 minutes. Remove from the heat and allow to cool for a few minutes. Turn the mixture into the pastry case and spread evenly. Roll out the remaining pastry and lay over the fruit. Dampen the edges of the pastry with a little milk and pinch well together. Brush the top with milk, dust with the demerara sugar and bake for 25–30 minutes, until the pastry is golden. Remove from the oven and leave to cool in the tin. When cold, cut into pieces and remove carefully from the tin.

NORFOLK TART

Norfolk is more famous for its use of honey in desserts and cakes than for syrup tarts, but this syrup- and-cream-based recipe makes a teatime treat. Honey has been a local product in the county for hundreds of years, especially at Walsingham, where the monks kept colonies of bees.

175g (6oz) rich shortcrust
    pastry (see page 90)
100g (4oz) golden syrup
15g (½oz) butter
Grated rind of half a lemon
2 tablespoons double cream
1 egg

Makes 1 x 18cm (7in)
round tart

Make the pastry following the instructions on page 90 and chill for at least 15 minutes. Preheat the oven to 200°C, 400°F, gas mark 6. Grease an 18cm (7in) round flan tin or dish. On a floured board, roll out the pastry to make a circle and use to line the prepared tin or dish. Bake blind for 15–20 minutes (see page 89). Remove from the oven and lift out the baking beans and paper. Reduce the oven temperature to 180°C, 350°F, gas mark 4. Warm the syrup in a pan with the butter and lemon rind until the butter has dissolved. Beat the cream and egg together and add to the mixture. Pour into the pastry case and bake for 20 minutes until golden and firm. Remove from the oven and serve warm or cold, or as a dessert with whipped or clotted cream.

SUCCESSFUL BAKING

INGREDIENTS

FLOUR

- **Plain flour** is generally used when little rise is required; for example, in pastries and shortbreads. To convert plain flour to self-raising flour, add baking powder in the quantities recommended on the container for different types of baking.
- **Self-raising flour** is used for cakes that need a raising agent. In some recipes, however, the amount of raising agent already added to the flour may be too great, so a mixture of plain and self-raising flour is used.
- Always store flour in a cool, dry place, preferably in an airtight container. Sift to remove any lumps and also to incorporate extra air before adding to the cake mixture.

RAISING AGENTS

- **Baking powder** is the most commonly used raising agent. It gives off carbon dioxide, which forms bubbles in the mixture. These expand during cooking, making the cake, scone or biscuit rise and helping to produce a light texture. Too much baking powder can cause sogginess and heaviness.
- **Bicarbonate of soda** is often used in recipes that include sour milk or buttermilk, spices, treacle and honey.
- **Sour milk** is sometimes necessary to give extra rise to heavy

mixtures, such as gingerbreads. It can be made at home by allowing milk to sit in a warm atmosphere until it curdles.

- **Buttermilk** is a standard ingredient in Welsh and Irish cookery and can be found in some supermarkets and from some milk-delivery companies.
- **Yeast** was once the only raising agent available for home baking, but is now generally used only in bread-making and in some traditional fruit or spice breads or pastries, such as saffron loaves, Chelsea buns and lardy cake. Dried yeast keeps for several months in an airtight container. Fresh yeast lasts for about a week in the refrigerator and will freeze for up to six months. Fresh yeast is often available from large supermarkets with bakeries, or local bakers. You may have to ask for it as it is not a 'shelf' item, but it is frequently free of charge.

  Dried or instant yeast can be substituted for fresh yeast. For 15g (½oz) fresh yeast use 6.25g (¼oz) dried or instant yeast, for 25g (1oz) fresh yeast use 10.5g (½oz) dried or instant yeast and for 50g (2oz) fresh yeast use 21g (¾oz) dried or instant yeast. If using dried yeast, dissolve in a little liquid of the recipe before adding to the other ingredients. If using instant yeast, add to the dry ingredients before mixing in the other ingredients. If using dried or instant yeast, the dough only needs to rise once.

FATS
- **Butter** and margarine are interchangeable in most recipes, but butter is preferable in shortbreads and rich fruit cakes, such as Christmas cake, that are to be stored for some time and matured before eating.
- **Lard** is often used in biscuits and gives a shorter texture.
- **Oil** is excellent in carrot cakes and chocolate cakes, and is ideal for anybody with a cholesterol problem.

- Allow butter, margarine or lard to soften to room temperature for at least an hour before using. Soft or whipped margarines can be used straight from the refrigerator.

EGGS
- Eggs should be at room temperature, as they are more likely to curdle if taken straight from the refrigerator.
- Small eggs (sizes 5 and 6) are too small for most recipes. Use large (sizes 1 and 2) or medium (sizes 3 and 4).

SUGAR AND OTHER SWEETENERS
- **Caster sugar** is generally used for creamed mixtures as it gives a much lighter texture than other types.
- **Granulated sugar** is acceptable in rubbed-in mixtures, but can produce a slightly gritty texture. It is worth paying a little extra for caster sugar.
- **Demerara sugar** is good in tea breads and in mixtures where ingredients are melted together, such as gingerbreads and boiled fruit cakes. It is excellent for sprinkling on the top of loaves and biscuits.
- **Soft brown sugar** gives a caramel flavour and beats well in creamed mixtures. The darker variety has a stronger flavour.
- **Black treacle** has a dark colour and strong flavour and is often used in gingerbreads and some fruit cakes.
- **Golden syrup** gives a soft, moist, sometimes sticky texture which is suitable for gingerbreads and flapjacks.
- **Honey** adds a very special distinctive flavour but too much will cause the mixture to burn easily.

PREPARING TINS

Most non-stick cake tins are very reliable if you follow the manufacturers' instructions but, to be on the safe side, it is wise to line and grease them anyway. Grease tins with whatever fat or oil is to be used in the recipe, then line with non-stick greaseproof parchment. Cut a single piece for the bottom of the tin and, when fitting paper to the sides, cut into the corners to make quite sure that it lies neatly against the tin. It may also be necessary to cut and overlap the paper, as the sides of circular tins sometimes slope slightly.

OVEN TEMPERATURES

Always make sure that the oven has reached the correct temperature before putting in the item to be baked. If you are not sure whether your oven is accurate, buy an oven thermometer and make regular checks. If using a convection oven, reduce all recommended temperatures by 20°C (68°F).

CAKES, SCONES AND BISCUITS

Always use the right tin for the recipe. Smaller or larger tins will affect the cooking time and hence the texture of the finished cake or biscuits.

Except in fan-assisted ovens, most cakes and biscuits cook best in the middle of the oven. Rich fruit cakes, large cakes and shortbreads should be placed just below the centre, and small, plain cakes, Swiss rolls and scones just above.

Do not disturb the cake during the first three-quarters of the baking time or, better still, not until you think it may be ready. Draughts and knocks can make the cake sink.

When placing biscuits on prepared tins, always allow room for them to spread during baking. It is better to leave too much room than to have all the biscuits merging into one misshapen mass.

IS IT READY?

To see if a sponge cake is ready, press lightly with a finger; if it springs back, it is cooked. To test fruitcakes and gingerbreads, stick a skewer into the middle of the cake and withdraw it immediately. If the skewer comes out clean, the cake is done. If not, allow a further 15 minutes and test again. Biscuits are usually ready when they are just turning golden. Scones are firm, well risen and golden when cooked.

If a cake begins to darken too quickly, place a double or triple layer of greaseproof paper over the top and continue cooking as usual.

PASTRY

The aim is to make pastry as light as possible, and this depends on how much cold air is trapped in the mixture before baking. The secret is to use cold ingredients, to have cold hands, cold bowls, a cold slab or surface on which to roll (marble is ideal) and to work in a cool room. Work quickly and lightly, using the fingertips when rubbing in, as too much handling makes the pastry tough. When rolling, sprinkle only a little flour on to the work surface and use light, even movements.

Most pastry recipes call for plain flour, but self-raising is sometimes used for suet crust and shortcrust. The more fat is used, the shorter the pastry will be; if the amount of fat is less than half the amount of flour, add 1 teaspoon of baking powder for each 225g (8oz) of flour. Butter, or butter mixed with lard, is best.

Rich pastry needs a hotter oven than others. If the oven is too cool, the fat will run out of the pastry and the pastry will be tough and chewy.

LINING PIE DISHES AND PLATES

Roll out the pastry to a thickness of about 0.25–0.5cm (⅛–¼in) and a little larger in size than the prepared dish or plate. Lay the pastry carefully on the dish, making sure that no air is trapped underneath. Do not stretch the pastry as it will only shrink back. If it is not big enough, roll out a little more and try again. Ease the pastry into all the rims and corners of the dish, then trim off any surplus. (Trimmings may be useful to make crosses on hot cross buns or a trellis over the top of a tart or pie.)

BAKING BLIND

This is necessary when an uncooked filling is to be put into the pastry case, or to set the pastry before any filling is poured in and cooked. When the prepared tin has been greased and lined with the pastry, prick the base all over with a fork. Cover the base with a piece of greaseproof paper followed by a layer of metal baking beans (available in any good cookware shop) or pasta or pulses (dried haricot beans, dried kidney beans or chickpeas). Bake in a preheated oven for just under the required time, then remove from the oven, lift out the baking beans and the greaseproof paper and bake for 5 minutes more to dry out the base.

PASTRY RECIPES

FLAKY PASTRY

450g (1lb) plain flour, sifted
1 teaspoon salt
350g (12oz) butter, or half
    butter and half lard, softened
1 teaspoon lemon juice
300ml (10fl oz) cold water

Mix together the flour and salt. Divide the fat into four portions. Rub one portion into the flour with your fingertips. Mix in the lemon juice and cold water to give a soft dough, rather like the consistency of butter. Knead gently on a lightly floured board until smooth. Roll out to a rectangle three times longer than it is wide. Dot the second portion of fat over the top two-thirds of the surface. Fold up the bottom third and fold down the top third and seal the edges by pressing together with a rolling pin. Wrap in clingfilm or a plastic bag and chill for 15 minutes. Place the dough on the floured board with the folded edges to your right and left, and roll out again to a rectangle. Repeat the dotting, folding and chilling process twice more until all the fat is used. Wrap again and chill for at least 45 minutes before using.

450g (1lb) plain flour, sifted
1 teaspoon salt
450g (1lb) butter, softened
1 teaspoon lemon juice
75–100ml (3–4fl oz) iced water

PUFF PASTRY

Mix together the flour and salt. Add 50g (2oz) of the butter, cut into small pieces, and rub into the flour until the mixture resembles fine breadcrumbs. Add the lemon juice and enough water to give a soft dough, similar to the consistency of butter. Knead lightly until really smooth. In a clean linen cloth, shape the remaining butter into a rectangle. On a lightly floured board, roll out the pastry to a rectangle slightly wider than the rectangle of butter and about twice its length. Place the butter on one half of the pastry and fold the other half over. Press the edges together with a rolling pin. Leave in a cool place for 15 minutes to allow the butter to harden slightly. Roll out the pastry to a long strip three times its original length, but keeping the width the same. The corners should be square, the sides straight and the thickness even. The butter must not break through the dough. Fold the bottom third up and the top third down, press the edges together with a rolling pin, put inside a well-oiled plastic bag and chill for 30 minutes. Place the dough on the floured board with the folded edges to your right and left, and roll out into a long strip as before. Fold again into three and chill for a further 30 minutes. Repeat this process four times more and chill for 30 minutes before using.

This is best made over two days, rolling three times and chilling overnight before completing the rolling the following day.

450g (1lb) plain flour, sifted
A good pinch of salt
350g (12oz) butter, softened
2 egg yolks
4 teaspoons caster sugar
3–4 tablespoons cold water

RICH SHORTCRUST PASTRY

Mix together the flour and salt. Rub in the butter until the mixture resembles breadcrumbs. Make a well in the middle, add the egg yolks and sugar and mix with a round-bladed knife. Add enough of the water, a little at a time, to give a stiff but pliable dough. Knead lightly until smooth. Wrap in clingfilm or a plastic bag and chill for at least 15 minutes before using.

450g (1lb) plain flour, sifted
A pinch of salt
350g (12oz) butter, softened
1 teaspoon lemon juice
3–4 tablespoons cold water

ROUGH PUFF PASTRY

Mix together the flour and salt. Cut the butter into small pieces and stir lightly into the flour with a round-bladed knife. Make a well in the middle, add the lemon juice and mix with enough water to give an elastic dough. On a lightly floured board, roll out the dough to a long strip, keeping the sides straight and the corners square. Fold up the bottom third and fold down the top third and turn the dough so that the folded edges are to your right and left. Repeat the rolling and folding process three times more, chilling the pastry for 15 minutes between the third and fourth rolling. Chill for at least 15 minutes before using.

450g (1lb) plain flour, sifted
A pinch of salt
100g (4oz) butter, softened
100g (4oz) lard, softened
3–4 tablespoons cold water

SHORTCRUST PASTRY

Mix together the flour and salt. Cut the fats into small pieces and rub into the flour until the mixture resembles fine breadcrumbs. Gradually add enough water, mixing with a fork, to give a stiff, but pliable dough. Knead lightly for a few minutes until smooth. Wrap in clingfilm or a plastic bag and chill for at least 15 minutes before using.

BREAD

FLOURS

The most commonly used flour for breadmaking is wheat. Strong wheat flour has a high gluten content and gives a better volume of bread, as it absorbs more water and makes a lighter dough. **White flour** is made from the starchy part of the grain from which the fibre and wheatgerm has been removed. **Wholewheat flour** is made from 100 per cent of the grain; nothing is added and nothing is taken away. **Wheatmeal** is made from 81–85 per cent of the grain and some of the fibre and wheatgerm has been removed.

Bread can be made with various other grains. **Rye** gives a dark dough and is usually mixed half and half with wheat flour; **barley** gives a cake-like texture and is usually mixed with wheat flour; maize gives a crumbly, crunchy texture. Other ingredients can be added to achieve different results: for example, extra bran, wheatgerm, sesame, poppy or sunflower seeds, cheese, herbs, spices, lemon or orange rind and rye flakes.

KNEADING

Kneading is an essential part of breadmaking as it helps to develop the gluten and the rise of the dough. Flour a board and use the palms of your hands, almost to the wrists, to push and turn the dough. As you work you can actually feel the texture changing to a smooth, elastic but not sticky consistency.

PROVING

Always cover the dough when setting it to prove; any draughts may affect the process. The yeast in the dough needs warmth to start working; the ideal temperature is between 36 and 44°C (98 and 110°F). Too much heat will kill the yeast; too little will stop it from working. The best place to leave dough to prove is on top of an Aga, a boiler or an active tumble dryer. The time taken for the dough to rise will depend on the warmth, but it usually takes 1–1½ hours. The second rising is quicker, usually between 20 minutes and half an hour.

BAKING SOLUTIONS

FRUIT CAKES

- If the fruit sinks to the bottom of the cake, it is probably because there was too little beating of fat and sugar, too much liquid or too much raising agent.
- If the cake sinks in the middle, it may be because the oven was not hot enough, or there was too little creaming of fat and sugar, or there was too much raising agent.

- If the cake is dry, it is usually because there was not enough liquid, or it is overcooked.
- If the top of the cake is cracked, the tin was too small and the oven was too hot.

SANDWICH AND SPONGE CAKES
- If the outside is too dark and the inside is not properly cooked, the oven was too hot and the cake was too near the top.
- If the top of the cake is domed, the oven was too hot or there was not enough beating.
- If the sponge does not rise well, there was either too little raising agent or the oven was too cool.

SCONES
- If the scones are tough, there was probably too much kneading.
- If the scones are hard and not spongy, there was too little liquid.
- If the scones are soggy in the middle, the oven was too cool or they were too low in the oven.
- If the scones have not risen, there was too little raising agent.

YEASTED BREADS AND CAKES
- If the loaf or cake is smaller than expected, there was either too much or too little raising agent, or the yeast did not activate properly due to incorrect temperature during proving.
- If the texture of the loaf or cake is coarse, the yeast was not properly mixed at the beginning, or there was too much yeast, which caused excessive rising and air in the dough.

INDEX

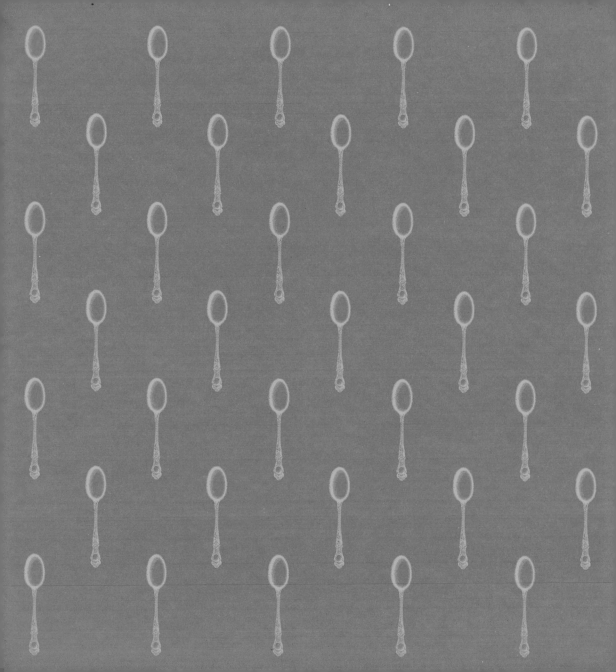